FORGIVE ME IF I WAS RUDE

FORGIVE ME IF I WAS RUDE

THE ART OF HAVING COMPLICATED, FAITH-BASED CONVERSATIONS

EMANUEL "DA' TRUTH" LAMBERT

DAVID C COOK
A MINISTRY OF COOK MEDIA GLOBAL

FORGIVE ME IF I WAS RUDE
Published by David C Cook
4050 Lee Vance Drive
Colorado Springs, CO 80918 U.S.A.

A Ministry of Cook Media Global

Integrity Music Limited, a Division of David C Cook
Brighton, East Sussex BN1 2RE, England

Library of Congress Control Number 2026934883
ISBN 978-0-8307-9220-7
eISBN 978-0-8307-9221-4

Published in association with The Bindery Agency, www.TheBinderyAgency.com.

The Team: Luke McKinnon, Jeff Gerke, Gina Pottenger, Brittany Stonestreet, Karen Sherry
Cover Design: James Hershberger
Cover Photo: Jason McCoy

Printed in the United States of America
First Edition 2026

1 2 3 4 5 6 7 8 9 10

070726

CONTENTS

FOREWORD

There's a tension every thoughtful Christian feels today: the desire to speak truth in love and the fear of saying the wrong thing in a world that seems ready to pounce on every word. We live in an age when conversations aren't just exchanges of ideas—they're battlegrounds for identity, morality, belonging, and even social dominance. The stakes are high, and the tone is often harsh. Nuance, especially on social media, is seen as compromise and then punished. In this climate, many believers retreat into silence, while others charge forward with zeal but little wisdom. One extreme never takes aim at the target, while the other misses the mark, sometimes wounding an innocent bystander.

That's why this book matters.

Emanuel Lambert—known to many as "Da' T.R.U.T.H."—has given us more than a manual for apologetics. He's given us a road map for grace-filled engagement in a fractured world. This isn't about winning arguments; it's about winning people. It's about learning to speak with compassion without sacrificing conviction. It's about holding fast to truth without letting go of humility. That is far easier to say than it is to do, of course. It requires more than clever words or airtight logic. It requires character, discernment, and dependence on the Holy Spirit.

I know this firsthand. Before I became a follower of Jesus, I was a committed Muslim. For nine years, I engaged in countless conversations with Christians who tried to share the gospel with me. Some conversations were respectful and thoughtful. Some conversations devolved into quarrels that produced more heat than light. Sometimes, that was my fault. I was determined to defend Islam and dismantle Christianity. Other times, the blame lay at the Christians' feet.

What ultimately changed me wasn't a single, powerfully articulated argument—it was credibility. I encountered Christians who knew not only what they believed but also how to communicate it. They listened—not just to my objections but to my concerns, my cares, my story. They listened more than they spoke, and when they did speak, their words carried weight because they were rooted in understanding and love. That posture made all the difference. It showed me that the gospel isn't just true; it's beautiful.

The framework Emanuel offers—affirmation, empathy, ask, answer—is deceptively simple. But don't mistake simplicity for superficiality. These four moves are deeply biblical and profoundly strategic. They mirror the way Jesus engaged people: affirming dignity, empathizing with pain, asking questions that expose the heart, and answering with truth that heals. In a world addicted to outrage, this approach feels almost revolutionary. It slows the pace, lowers the temperature, and opens the door for genuine dialogue.

But this book does more than teach technique. It calls us to become a certain kind of person. That's crucial, because the credibility of our message is tied to the integrity of our lives. Emanuel reminds us that holiness isn't about withdrawal from the world nor performance for the world—it's about love. Love that listens. Love that risks misunderstanding. Love that refuses to treat people as projects. If we miss that, our sharpest arguments will fall upon ears clogged with the wax of suspicion, resentment, and hurt. It would be a tragedy indeed, as the arguments for the gospel's credibility are too compelling to be wasted, and the people to whom we offer them are too precious to be mishandled.

That's why I appreciate Emanuel's emphasis on restraint. In an age of hot takes and instant replies, restraint feels counterintuitive. But sometimes faithfulness means holding back. It means resisting the urge to correct every error or comment on every thread. It means trusting that the Spirit is at work even when we're silent. That kind of restraint isn't weakness—it's wisdom. And wisdom is what this book offers in spades.

As you read, you'll find practical tools for navigating tough questions about suffering, sexuality, other religions, and more. You'll find insights on reading the room, understanding cultural narratives, and leveraging the power of story. But more than that, you'll find a vision for what it looks like to engage the world without losing your soul. A vision that says evangelism isn't a transaction; it's an act of love. A vision that says apologetics isn't about proving a point; it's about pointing to a Person.

If you're weary and leery of the shouting matches, if you're tired of conversations that turn into combat, if you long for a better way, this book is for you. It doesn't give you shortcuts or promise easy wins. But it will equip you to enter hard spaces with humility and hope. It will challenge you to depend on the Spirit, to cultivate character, and to speak truth with a tone that reflects the One who is Truth.

In the end, that's what our world needs—not just Christians who know what to say, but Christians who know how to say it. Not just defenders of the faith, but ambassadors of grace. Emanuel Lambert has shown us how. Now it's up to us to live it.

Abdu Murray,
speaker and author

Introduction

THE CHEAT CODE

The conversations we're having today aren't simple. Whether it's a coworker asking what you believe about gay marriage, a cousin wrestling with church hurt, a college professor mocking your faith, a friend bringing up crystals and "positive energy," or a stranger on TikTok confidently claiming that the Bible is full of contradictions, we are living in a time when nearly every conversation is complicated.

And there's tension in the air.

As Christians whose faith is often seen as outdated, intolerant, or tone deaf, we feel this tension every day. Culture wars are everywhere. Debates are constant. People are deconstructing, unfollowing, and unfriending. Language is shifting. Norms are evolving. Emotions are high. And the line between disagreement and disrespect feels razor thin.

In the midst of all this, we find ourselves not only in the crosshairs of the culture but also carrying within our very bodies the anticipatory anxiety of being asked a religious question we don't have the answer to or being confronted with an idea we haven't thought through.

We want to say something. We want to represent Jesus well. We want to respond thoughtfully. These conversations are incredible opportunities to stand for your Lord and to possibly help someone down the path toward an outcome that will change their eternity, not only for the person you're engaging with but also for the many who are watching it unfold online. But sometimes—whether it's at school or work or simply when logging into social media—we just don't feel prepared.

That's why I wrote this book.

Forgive Me If I Was Rude is here to help you, so you can know not only what to say in those scenarios but also how to say it. How can you take what comes to you in the form of an attack or accusation against your faith and turn it into something that can bring the other person into a new state of receptivity to the gospel?

In my experience, a lot of books in this "apologetics" genre lean heavily into the academic side (big concepts, complex ideas, and thought-provoking theories), but they never really land in everyday life. That's not the kind of book I want to give you. I want you to see what these important conversations can look like in real life. So in each chapter, I've included a section where I walk you through an actual conversation, step by step.

What to say. What not to say. How to respond wisely without overreacting. How to hold your convictions without shutting people down.

The Cheat Code

Just so we're clear, when I call this the "cheat code," I'm not talking about skipping the work or bypassing real understanding. I'm giving you a tool, a handy framework for navigating hard conversations, that makes these exchanges more manageable, so you're not left scrambling when the moment hits you.

What I'm offering here is structure. Language. A framework you can lean on when the pressure is real and the conversation is moving fast. I'm not telling you *what* to think. I'm helping you with *how* to respond, *how* to frame the moment, and *how* to move the conversation forward without panic or posturing.

Think of this equipping as a set of ready-to-use handles and phrases, approaches and responses to difficult questions that give you footing when emotions are high and clarity is hard to find. You're not walking into these moments empty-handed; you're walking in prepared, with tools already in your pocket.

The goal isn't to make you sound scripted. It's to help you stay present, grounded, and thoughtful, so instead of reacting on impulse, you can respond with intention.

Over my years of engaging with people in these scenarios, both in person and online, I began to notice something. The conversations that went well, the ones that opened doors instead of closing them, had a consistent rhythm. There was a pattern hidden inside those moments where tension dissolved and understanding began to form.

That's what led to the four-part sequence you're about to learn. Think of this as a set of rails you can ride when the moment catches you off guard. It's not a script. It's scaffolding—a flexible structure that keeps your posture grounded, your tone gentle, and your answers both truthful and accessible.

Now let's look at this framework and how it works.

We'll start with the *objection* or *accusation* the other person (who is beloved by God) brings. We'll look at the knee-jerk *rude response* we're tempted to fire off. And then we'll start crafting a *better response.*

Let's imagine a scenario in which someone says to you, "I don't see anything wrong with using crystals or sage. It's all good energy."

Okay, that's the person's *objection*. The objection is a statement, belief, or critique raised against the Christian worldview.

Most likely, some quick answer will probably come to your mind. In this case, maybe you find yourself wanting to fire back with, "Just because you don't see anything wrong with it doesn't mean it's good."

That's what I call the *rude response*. It's almost always an example of what not to say. It may be your first impulse, but it's usually blunt, unhelpful, or prematurely confrontational. This person has given you a question or challenge that could end up being the lifeline that leads to the salvation of their eternal soul, but the rude response may send them away, and perhaps they won't give anyone else the opportunity they gave you.

Now let's look at the better response. It has four elements: affirm, empathize, ask, and answer—AEAA.

When you *affirm*, you find the understandable or relatable part of what the person said. In our example about crystals, you might affirm like this: "I get it. A lot of people are looking for peace, healing, and clarity. That makes total sense."

Compare that with the rude response. With affirmation, you're immediately turning their sword into a plowshare. They came at you with an attack, or at least with an idea you know to be wrong, but rather than batting it away and putting them in their place with "truth," you're receiving it without taking offense.

You're also affirming where they're coming from. I'm convinced that most of what people are looking for when they speak is to find out if they're going to be safe to express what they're thinking. An affirmation like this gives them the feeling that they're in a protected space, and maybe now some actual dialogue can begin.

Next you *empathize*. Here, you seek to identify the fear, pain, shared humanity, and common ground that is possibly behind their statement, and you express compassion for the person. Something like, "Life can feel chaotic and heavy, so it makes total sense that you want something to help you feel centered or protected. Listen, come on: I'm like you. I want what you want. Because the truth is that these longings and desires are embedded in the soul of every human being."

With empathy, you enter their world emotionally and validate the human longing beneath their comment. This is crucial to getting to the heart of what's really being said.

And isn't this how God is with us? We come to Him with all kinds of wrong ideas and wacky thoughts. Imagine if He shot off a rude response to us. Imagine if He couldn't see through our question to our true fear and need. Pray for the Lord to give you eyes to see their true need and ears to hear their true hurt.

The next step is to *ask* a question. Offer an open-ended, non-defensive question that invites honest dialogue. In our example, maybe it could be something like, "What brought you to this place where you felt like crystals or sage helped meet your spiritual needs? What do they give you that you've been looking for?"

Really listen to the person's answer. Maybe ask follow-up questions. If you show authentic interest in their thoughts and opinions, giving them the chance to express them in a receptive dialogue, you earn the right to offer your thoughts too.

Which brings us to the final step in the four-part sequence: your *answer*.

Here's the payoff for the work you've done so far. Offer a concise, respectful articulation of the Christian belief on the topic. For our scenario, it might be, "From a Christian perspective, we believe peace and healing are found through the presence of God Himself, not energy or objects. And sometimes practices that seem harmless can actually open doors we didn't intend to walk through. I'd love to talk more about what that means if you're open to it."

See how it works? And do you see what a good and useful spot the conversation has moved to? What if you'd shot off that rude answer? It might have been a true statement, but carving "TRUTH" into your baseball bat and bludgeoning someone with it may not be the path to fruitful conversation about the Lord.

Affirm, empathize, ask, answer—AEAA. Maybe an acronym will help: An Elephant Ate Andy (sorry, Andy).

These conversations often go to two or more rounds. Let's say the person you're speaking with has listened to your AEAA words so far, and now they have a follow-up comment. It's a second objection, or we might call it a rebuttal. Something like this, maybe: "Yeah, I hear you. I've heard that before. But I feel like Christians think anything outside of Christianity is automatically dangerous. Just because something's different doesn't mean it's evil."

You have to watch yourself, because even now you might have a new rude response pop into your mind. Remember to form a better response with the AEAA pattern. Here's an example.

Affirm

That's a fair point. Christians definitely have a reputation for that.

Empathize

And listen, if something seems to be working, why wouldn't you stick with it? I get it. That makes sense too.

Ask

Do you think there's a line between what's spiritually helpful and what's spiritually harmful? And if so, how do we know which is which?

Answer

First of all, thank you for talking to me about this. My thought is that the reason we outsource our spiritual needs is because we're all looking for peace, protection, clarity, wisdom, and control. These longings are embedded in every human soul. Practices like sage and crystals promise a sense of groundedness. But from the biblical perspective, Jesus is our Wonderful Counselor, Mighty God, and Prince of Peace (Isa. 9:6 BSB). He doesn't just offer those things ... He is those things. And the difference is that He's personal. He doesn't just give us clarity; He walks with us in confusion. He doesn't just give us peace; He is peace, present with us in the storm. And you don't have to burn sage to access Him.

Possible Dialogue

Them—Objection

Do you believe atheists go to hell?

You—Rude Response

You just better hope you don't go to hell. Nah, I'm just playin'.

Why This Doesn't Work

Even if it's meant to be humorous, a sarcastic or defensive response can shut the conversation down, reinforce stereotypes, or sound like you're deflecting from a serious issue. This is a question that deserves both honesty and compassion.

Better Response (The AEAA Approach to Bridge Building)

You—Affirm

I'm assuming you're asking this from a posture of seeking fairness. Like, if the answer is yes, that just feels wrong or unjust.

Empathize

And if that's what's underneath your question, I totally get it. There are a lot of people, even within the Christian faith, who wrestle with the same thing.

Ask

So let me ask you this: If it were true that an atheist goes to hell, what would that say about God, in your view? Or what would it say about Christianity?

Answer

As a disclaimer, I want to say that God didn't create hell for people. Neither does He take any pleasure in anyone going there. But at the same time, Jesus did teach that anyone who rejects Him will spend eternity separated from the Father. Yes, the Bible does call that separation hell.

Them—Rebuttal

Well, if you believe that, then you're intolerant.

You—Affirm

Okay, I hear you. And I understand why it comes off that way.

Empathize

Even as a Christian, I've had moments where I've wrestled with the narrowness of my faith.

Ask

When you say Christianity is intolerant, do you mean because it makes exclusive truth claims? If so, isn't that what you're doing too? When you say God is unfair or Christians are intolerant, those are also truth claims.

Answer

That's important to acknowledge because it actually levels the playing field. Since we're both making exclusive claims about what's true, the real questions become: Which claim actually makes sense of the world? Which one is grounded in reality, love, justice, and truth? If I'm wrong, I want to know. But if it's true, then it matters more than anything.

Why This Book Matters

Shhh, don't tell anybody, but this book is kind of like the CliffsNotes for complicated conversations. The "never be stumped again" guide. The pocket-sized "Wait, what do I say to that?" handbook. This book is for real life.

It's meant to help you feel more prepared, to give you quick, clear answers when the moment catches you off guard. The kind of book you can flip through before work, after class, or right before that tough family convo.

But it's not just about having answers. It's also about being able to step into any conversation confident in what you believe, wise in how you say it, and full of grace in how you carry yourself.

Because the more prepared you are, the better your chances of removing barriers that hinder people from having a clear understanding of who God is.

It isn't about winning arguments. It's about building bridges and letting the beauty of the gospel shine through, both in what you say and how you say it.

I've heard some people say, "We don't need more knowledge, we don't need more debate tactics, and we don't need more apologetics. We don't need more arguments. What we need is more love."

And while that might sound noble, I believe it's a false choice. Because it's not either/or. It's both/and. *The truth is, we do need arguments.* Not the kind rooted in combativeness or contentiousness, but the kind rooted in clarity, reasoning, and thoughtful engagement.

In fact, the entire Christian story has been preserved, clarified, protected, and strengthened through argument ... meaningful, reasoned, Spirit-guided dialogue.

To argue, in the classical sense, simply means to make a case. It doesn't mean to be quarrelsome or contentious. It means to engage the mind God gave us—to compare, discern, examine, and articulate what is true.

Scripture itself is full of arguments:

- The prophets argued with Israel, reasoning with them on God's behalf (Isa. 1:18; Jer. 2:9; Mic. 6:1–2; Mal. 3:7–10).
- Jesus engaged in arguments constantly—not to fight but to reveal truth.
- Matthew structured his entire Gospel as an argument that Jesus is the Messiah (1:1–17; 1:22–23; 2:5–6; 5–7).
- Paul used reasoning in person and nearly every letter he wrote was an extended argument—anticipating objections, answering critics, building a case point by point (Acts 17:2–3; Rom. 1–11; 1 Cor. 15).
- The writer of Hebrews constructed one of the most sophisticated arguments in the entire biblical canon about the supremacy of Christ (1:1–4; 7–10).

And after the apostles, the early church continued the pattern. The church fathers didn't preserve the faith through sensationalism—they preserved it *through councils, debates, careful reasoning, and doctrinal arguments that clarified what Christians actually believe.*

- The Council of Nicaea was an argument.[1]
- The Council of Chalcedon was an argument.
- The canonization of Scripture required *decades* of argument.[2]

These weren't petty fights. They were necessary conversations that protected the church from distortion and united believers around truth.

Even the spiritual gift of teaching is rooted in this idea. Teachers don't just explain—*they argue.* They compare Scripture with Scripture. They refute error. They persuade. They help the church think clearly. Teaching is part of the "fivefold ministry," a gift God gave to the body not simply to inspire hearts but to shape minds (see Eph. 4:11–13).

To say, "We don't need more arguments; we just need more love," is to misunderstand both love *and* argument.

Because biblical love tells the truth.

And biblical truth is meant to be explained, defended, reasoned, and shared.

It's not love *versus* clarity.

It's not love *versus* apologetics.

It's not love *versus* conviction.

It's love that speaks truth, and truth that's spoken in love.

That's exactly what the apostle Peter said. Peter was writing to Jewish and Gentile Christians scattered across the Roman Empire who were living under increasing persecution and cultural hostility. Their faith made them outsiders, often misunderstood and maligned.

And yet Peter urges them to be ready to speak, to defend their hope, but to do so *with gentleness and respect.* He didn't say, "Don't speak," and he didn't say, "Don't defend." He said, "Do it right."

> Always be prepared to give an answer to everyone who asks you to give the reason for the hope that you have. But do this with gentleness and respect. (1 Pet. 3:15 NIV)

Giving an answer (or defense)—that's knowing what to say.

Doing it with gentleness and respect—that's knowing how to say it.

It's truth and love. Clarity and compassion. Boldness and grace. These aren't mutually exclusive or opposing values. They're complementary. It's like how Paul told us to speak the truth in love (Eph. 4:15).

Jesus didn't command us only to love God and love people. He also told us to love God *with our minds.* That means having a faith that is informed, one that requires thinking deeply, engaging honestly, and preparing to give thoughtful, meaningful answers when it matters most.

This book exists to help you do exactly that.

Chapter 1

THE ARENA

To be relevant we must first understand the questions our culture is asking.

Tim Keller, ***Center Church***

Before soldiers enter battle, their commanders study the terrain. They don't march in blind, hoping courage alone will be enough. They send scouts. They study maps. They ask questions like: What's the ground like? Where are the choke points? Where's the high ground? In today's world, commanders send drones and consult satellite imagery to do reconnaissance before the first soldier ever moves.

The same is true for boxers in the ring. Before they throw a punch, they bounce on the canvas, test the ropes, and get a feel for the space they're about to sweat and bleed in. Because knowing the ring matters. The canvas can be soft or firm. The ropes can be loose or tight. The corners can feel wide or cramped. All those small details can change the rhythm of the fight. Boxers who know the ring have an edge before the first bell even sounds because they've already studied the environment where every punch, dodge, and step will play out.

In the same way, we can't rush into these complicated conversations "guns blazing" with one-size-fits-all answers. Our job is reconnaissance, to survey the land, to read the terrain, to know the ring. Having a feel for the environment where the "fight" will play out gives us an edge before we ever speak. Because if we don't understand the environment, we'll end up throwing knives in a gunfight or, as Andy Stanley would say, giving "faith-based answers to fact-based questions."[1]

The apostle Paul is a great example of someone who always knew the arena he was stepping into. When he wrote letters to the churches, they were never generic. When he sat down to write to the church in Corinth, he already knew their city was a hub of commerce and corruption, a place obsessed with status and speechmaking. When he wrote to the Galatians, he understood the pull of legalism. Speaking in Athens, he read the terrain: a city obsessed with knowledge, forever chasing the "new idea." Paul always had his finger on the pulse of the culture he was stepping into.[2]

What Are We Stepping Into?

For us in the West, especially in the United States, the arena is a mixed bag. We are a democracy, a self-proclaimed melting pot, a nation that prides itself on diversity of thought, belief, culture, and conscience. There isn't only one worldview to engage with, but dozens. That means the battle, or the conversation, looks different depending on where you are and who you're with.

So if we're going to engage in this arena, here's what we need to know about the ground we're stepping onto.

Our "ring" is a world where hedonism has taken root. Pleasure has been enthroned as the highest good. Social media glamorizes indulgence, flex culture, hookup culture, cosmetic surgeries, and transactional relationships where sex is traded for money and money for sex. Pleasure isn't just permitted; it's expected. And yet beneath all the glitter resides a deep restlessness that pleasure cannot satisfy.

One of my favorite quotes from Chuck Swindoll is "The moment you get the thing you've always wanted, it only creates a desire for more of what you don't have."[3]

We are living in a culture where asceticism also exerts a pull. If hedonism says, "More is better," asceticism whispers, "Less will save you." It's the opposite instinct, the stripping down of life to its barest simplicity. You see it in the rise of minimalism, wellness culture, eco-spirituality, and the "ascetic lifestyle" trend of neutral tones, soft lighting, and quiet spaces.

It's fascinating when you think about it. I recently came across a live clip of Willow Smith saying she couldn't understand how people weren't living an ascetic lifestyle.[4] Since she comes from a family of wealth and global recognition, you might expect her to lean toward extravagance. Instead, her public posture is stripped down, minimalistic, and intentionally understated. She's emblematic of a generation weary of excess, disenchanted with consumerism, and drawn to simplicity as salvation.

And yet, even that impulse carries a kind of spirituality of its own. Beneath the language of "alignment," "energy," and "vibration" is a worldview that still seeks redemption, just without a Redeemer. It's spirituality without Christ, purity without grace, and peace without surrender. What looks harmless on the surface, a pursuit of balance and calm, often masks the same hunger every other worldview is chasing: the need to be made whole.

At the same time, we inhabit a society swimming in relativism. Like the Greeks, we've made man the measure of all things.[5] To us, truth is a matter of taste, not fact. Morality is a matter of preference, not principle. On the surface, that sounds tolerant and inclusive—everyone gets to choose what's right for them. But the moment you disagree, you discover how intolerant relativism really is.

It's in this climate that George Orwell's chilling image of 2 + 2 = 5 doesn't seem so far-fetched anymore.[6] Relativism has created a climate where even the most absurd ideas can not only survive but thrive. The soil is ripe for it. We hear phrases like "math is racist" or "men can get pregnant." In another age, such claims would have sounded ridiculous. Today, they're debated on talk shows, argued in classrooms, and legislated into policy. Relativism has tilled the ground so thoroughly that 2 + 2 = 5 no longer sounds like dystopian fiction—it's just Tuesday.

Layered on all this is the power of popular culture, which disciples more effectively than most preachers. TikTok, Instagram, Netflix, and hip-hop are the new catechisms. Our artists carry the philosophies of our age. Kendrick Lamar gives us social activism. Drake baptizes indulgence. Murder music recycles stereotypes of violence. Pop stars preach existentialism: Make your own meaning, break your own rules. Add to that the materialism flaunted online—luxury brands and bags and shoes as well as cosmetically enhanced bodies—and you see what really shapes this generation. Most people don't realize they're being indoctrinated; they think they're just being entertained.

All of this bleeds directly into questions about faith and belonging. Religion and identity in America have left us a fractured and complicated inheritance. Christianity has been liberator and oppressor, fuel for abolition and weapon for slaveholders. This soiled history has left deep wounds. Many African Americans, disillusioned with Christianity's complicity in oppression, are turning back to African spirituality, mysticism, or ancestral practices. Others walk away into cynicism or unbelief. Religion is not a unifier here; it's a tainted legacy.

Out of that history has emerged a wave of deconstruction. A generation raised in the church is walking away. Some are disillusioned by hypocrisy. Others are scarred by abuse or exhausted by political entanglement. Still others wrestle with intellectual doubts never taken seriously. They are not atheists by default; they are shipwrecked believers, wounded wanderers, carrying fragments of faith but unsure what to do with them.

Most people don't realize they're being indoctrinated; they think they're just being entertained.

Beneath it all runs a deeper reality: a spiritual current. Paul said it plainly: We wrestle not against flesh and blood (Eph. 6:12). The spirit of the antichrist (1 John 4:3) whispers through every false version of Jesus—Islam denying His divinity, Hebrew Israelism (not Judaism but a modern movement whose members call themselves Black Israelites) distorting His identity, secularism reducing Him to "just a teacher." The "doctrines of demons" (1 Tim. 4:1) give us teachings that sound enlightened but are designed to deceive: relativism that erodes truth, mysticism that replaces Christ with energy or ancestors, and prosperity gospels that make God a means to an end.

The contradictions we see in our culture don't float on their own; they are carried by a current deeper than most people can see. As Paul wrote, "The god of this age has blinded the minds of unbelievers" (2 Cor. 4:4 NIV). What happens in the culture is never just natural; it is always spiritual at the root.

But those spiritual currents don't stay invisible. They show up in our schools, in our government, in our churches, and most visibly now in the digital public square.

What is the public square?

For centuries, the public square was a literal place. It was the plaza in a European city where people gathered to trade, to argue, to protest, and to worship.

It was the street corners of Philadelphia, where I remember standing surrounded by city noise, both observing and engaging in conversations about God, politics, and culture. The debates were intense. Voices clashed, tensions rose to the boiling point, and yet the crowd leaned in, listening with rapt attention. The air was charged. It was the kind of space where you could feel the weight of the ideas in the atmosphere.

Today, the public square still exists, but it has expanded. It's no longer confined to the plaza or the street corner. It's global now, and it has relocated to social media. The public square has gone digital. The same energy that once filled marketplaces and corners now lives on TikTok, YouTube, X, and Instagram.[7]

That's where the audience is too. The same listening crowd that once gathered shoulder to shoulder in the streets is now gathered on screens, swiping and scrolling, watching every exchange in real time.

That means the arena we step into is not only ideological but is also technological. The debates, the culture wars, the questions of faith and identity, all of it now plays out in the digital public square. Social media is the new center of discourse, the new arena of engagement.

I'll go deeper into this in the next chapter, but for now it's enough to recognize this: The fight for truth and wisdom is not only about what or who we're engaging but also where.

How Did We Get Here?

In a recent conversation, I found myself sitting in the backyard under the hot Louisiana sun, talking with members of my family, John and Shelly, about the state of the culture. We touched on everything: the divisiveness, race relations, the tension you can almost feel in the air. Midway through the conversation, John leaned up in his chair and asked a question I wasn't expecting: "But how did we get here?"

It's such an important question. How did we get from the sexual conservatism of the 1950s—where sexuality was hushed, hidden, and bound by rules—to the hedonism of today, where pleasure is enthroned and hookup culture is celebrated? How did we get from a society that once prided itself on science, empiricism, and the pursuit of objective truth, to a relativistic worldview where 2 + 2 = 5 can be debated in classrooms and morality is treated as preference instead of principle? How did we get from a culture where most Americans identified as Christian, even if only nominally, to a place where, particularly among African Americans, there's often open disdain for Christianity because of its soiled history with slavery, racism, and hypocrisy?

The truth is that none of this is random. What we're living through now is the culmination of centuries of fracture, cultural experiments, and spiritual deception. Major cultural shifts never happen in a vacuum.

They almost never happen overnight. Instead, they unfold slowly, across generations, and they usually take the form of overcorrections. One generation looks back at the mistakes of the previous generation and tries to fix them, but in the process, they swing too far in the opposite direction. The pendulum doesn't just swing—it lurches.[8]

Take sexuality, for example. In the 1950s, sex was treated as shameful to mention. Families didn't talk about it. Churches reduced it to rules and prohibitions. Society reinforced silence around the subject. The next generation reacted. The sexual revolution of the 1960s swung the pendulum hard the other way, fueled by the birth control pill, countercultural rebellion, and a rising distrust of authority. What had once been hushed became flaunted. Music and movies, and more recently MTV and the internet, normalized what the previous generation had tried to suppress. What began as correction turned into overcorrection—and the result is hedonism.

One generation looks back at the mistakes of the previous generation and tries to fix them, but swings too far in the opposite direction.

The same thing happened with truth. For centuries, the West leaned heavily on objective truth: science, reason, empiricism. But there was a rigidity to it, and truth was often wielded like a weapon. The next generation reacted. Postmodern thinkers questioned whether truth could ever really be known or if it was a tool of the powerful. That suspicion filtered down into culture, and soon "my truth" replaced the truth. Millennials embraced subjectivity, relabeling it as authenticity. Gen Z doubled down, declaring that to question someone's lived truth was to commit an act of harm.

What started as a correction to cold rationalism became an overcorrection into full-blown relativism. Now relativism thrives.

And that's the point: Nothing happens in a vacuum. Shifts don't appear out of thin air. They unfold over time, through generations reacting to one another, trying to fix what came before but often going too far. That's how we got here. And if we're going to engage this moment with wisdom, we need to understand where we are, because context doesn't just inform us—it equips us.

CURIOUS CONVERSATION

"What's true for you isn't true for me."

Forgive Me If I Was Rude is about learning to engage the culture wisely and compassionately, understanding not only what people believe but also why they believe it. In this chapter, we have been exploring the arena we're stepping into—a world shaped by philosophies like hedonism, materialism, and relativism.

And while each of these influences plays a part in shaping our generation, few are as pervasive (or as subtle) as relativism. It's everywhere. It shapes how Westerners think about truth, morality, God, and even themselves. It's the lens through which most modern people view life, the unspoken assumption behind so many of our conversations.

That's why I've devoted this chapter's Curious Conversation to relativism. Because if we don't know how to talk about truth in a world that treats truth like a feeling, then we'll keep missing the deeper issue beneath almost every debate.

Possible Dialogue

Them—Objection

Truth is relative. What's true for you isn't necessarily true for me. What works for you works for you, and what works for me works for me.

You—Rude Response

I hear you, but that just doesn't make any sense.

Why This Doesn't Work

It comes off as dismissive, shuts the door on dialogue, and makes the other person feel belittled. Even if you're right, it guarantees they'll stop listening.

Better Response

You—Affirm

I get why that feels appealing: It sounds open-minded and freeing.

Empathize

Honestly, who wouldn't want to live that way? Make your own rules, live how you want—it sounds good on the surface.

Ask

But can I ask: Does it really work that way? Or does it end up in regret and chaos in your life?

Answer

I really want you to think about this. If everybody lives by their own personal definition of what truth is, or what *good* is, how could there ever be justice in the world?

If a criminal act were committed against you or someone you love, and the case went to trial, "personal truth" wouldn't bring justice. Imagine if the witness on the stand actually saw the crime happen but decided to lie about it. In a relativistic world, how could you even call that a lie? Or perhaps the person who committed the crime is fully convinced that the ends justify the means, operating with a kind of Robin Hood logic, telling themselves they were only robbing from the "unworthy" rich in order to give to the "deserving" poor.

If everyone defines truth or goodness for themselves, then there's no standard for honesty, no foundation for justice, and no way to call anything wrong. The moment we say, "What works for you works for you," we've lost the ability to say that anything is unjust. Without an objective standard, truth and justice collapse.

Them—Rebuttal 1

But if you don't let people define their own truth, and you impose your truth onto them, isn't that oppression?

You—Affirm

I get that concern; it's a fair question. Nobody wants to feel controlled or silenced. The fear of oppression is real, especially when we've seen religion or power used in manipulative ways.

Empathize

I understand why the idea of defining your own truth feels like freedom. On the surface, it sounds like the most compassionate and liberating approach: Everyone gets to choose what's right for themselves without judgment.

Ask

But what if the opposite is true? What if relativism—the idea that everyone creates their own truth—actually produces more oppression, not less?

Answer

Think about it: Without objective standards of right and wrong, we lose any fixed moral foundation. There are no boundaries, no guardrails, no transcendent principles to guide us. When "truth" becomes fluid, power or maybe even violence fills the vacuum. Whoever has the loudest voice, the most influence, or the biggest platform becomes the new moral authority.

History shows that when societies abandon absolute standards, confusion always follows. The French Revolution promised liberation from moral restraint but quickly devolved into the Reign of Terror.

The Soviet Union, built on the idea that morality was determined by the state, led to the oppression and death of millions. Even in modern times, when morality becomes subjective, injustice multiplies. What's considered virtuous one decade becomes "hateful" the next.

The consequences are just as real at the personal level. A 2023 study from the American Psychological Association found that Gen Z, often called the most relativistic generation, also reports the highest rates of anxiety and depression in U.S. history. Nearly nine out of ten Gen Z adults say they feel stressed or uncertain about life's purpose. When there's no higher standard to anchor us, no meaning beyond our moods, we end up untethered and exhausted.[9]

Relativism promises freedom but delivers exhaustion. It tells us to create our own meaning but leaves us with none. It claims to liberate us from judgment, but it ends up enslaving us to comparison, confusion, and chaos.

Them—Rebuttal 2

I hear you. I just can't have anybody telling me how to live my life.

You—Affirm

Yeah, that's how we all feel, to be honest. All of us, including myself, would love it if we could just make up our own rules and live the way we want to live without any accountability.

Empathize

I think it's natural to feel that way.

Ask

I'm always curious, though, about how that works out. It seems like every time I've tried to do that—just go my own way, live my own life, make my own rules—it doesn't end well. How do you feel that's worked out for you?

Answer

Here's the thing: I don't know if you believe this or not, but as a Christian, I personally believe that I was *created*. I didn't come into existence by accident or happenstance. I'm not the product of a random process. I was created by a personal, powerful, intelligent Being, a creator we call God.

God, as our creator, knows exactly how we're wired and what leads to our flourishing. His commands aren't arbitrary; they're protective.

And if God is our creator and designer, then He should have the final say in how we live our lives. The same way that the designers of an iPhone or a MacBook understand the functionality of what they made, God understands the purpose and design of His creation. Apple engineers know how their devices are meant to function, and that's why they install safeguards and codes. Not to limit you but to protect the integrity of the design—to keep it from being corrupted or damaged.

The same is true with us. God, as our creator, knows exactly how we're wired and what leads to our flourishing. His commands aren't arbitrary; they're protective. Just like traffic lights and stop signs, His rules don't exist to keep us from getting where we need to go—they exist to keep us from crashing. A red light isn't there to frustrate you; it's there to preserve your life and the lives of others.

So when God sets boundaries and tells us how to live, it's not meant to restrict us—it's meant to protect us. His boundaries don't rob us of freedom; they make freedom possible.

KEYS FOR THE CONVERSATION

Every chapter has a lot of moving pieces, but if you can remember these keys, you'll carry the heart of this chapter and the tools you'll need into every conversation.

1. What You Need to Know

You can't have wise conversations if you don't understand the environment you're stepping into. Modern culture is shaped by hedonism, relativism, materialism, digital influence, spiritual confusion, and generational wounds. Before you speak, you must know the terrain.

2. What You Need to Do

Study the culture you're living in. Research the rooms you're stepping into. Depending on how far you want to go, that can mean paying attention to pop culture, cultural trends, and online conversations, or going deeper—delving into sociology, history, generational dynamics, and worldview formation.

Before you speak, study the climate:

- Is the room warm? Cold? Stiff? Stoic? Familiar? Unfamiliar?
- Is there 0 percent relational equity or 80 percent?

Understanding the room will guide how you engage.

And as you study, apply Paul's posture: Affirm where you can affirm. Find common ground through shared language and familiar points of connection. Be intentional and strategic so that every bridge you build can ultimately lead people toward Jesus.

3. Who You Need to Become

Become a person who takes context seriously.

Someone who understands that environments are not one-size-fits-all and that every room requires humility, attention, and discernment.

Become a student—like the descendants of Issachar who "understood the times and knew what Israel should do" (1 Chron. 12:32 NIV). Scripture shows repeatedly that times, seasons, and moments matter, and the Holy Spirit speaks expressly into them. So become someone who honors context, listens deeply, and discerns what faithfulness looks like right where you stand.

Chapter 2

WHO DO YOU THINK YOU'RE TALKING TO?

To know how to respond, you must first know who stands before you.

Stephen R. Covey, *The 7 Habits of Highly Effective People: Powerful Lessons in Personal Change*

When you hear the phrase "Who do you think you're talking to?" it's usually not a good thing.

Most of the time, it's said in the middle of an argument: heated, confrontational, and often laced with attitude. Sometimes, you might hear it framed a little differently: "I don't know who you think you're talking to, but ..." Either way, it's rarely a favorable exchange. It's a statement meant to challenge, to put someone in check, to demand respect.

That's how it's usually used.

But taken literally, it's a crucial question, especially when it comes to deep, difficult, or controversial conversations.

Because if you don't take the time to understand who you're engaging with, how can you expect to connect with them in a meaningful way?

Complicated conversations (or as we'll refer to them in this book, *curious* conversations) require more than knowledge; they also require awareness of the person in front of you, their perspective, and the experiences that have shaped the way they see the world.

If we want to have meaningful conversations (especially about faith), we can't afford to be careless with our approach. It's not just about delivering the right information. It's about knowing who's on the other side of it.

In the previous chapter, we stepped into the arena. That was about the *where*. The where deals with context—the climate, culture, and background noise that shape the conversation. But this chapter is about the who. The who is different. The *who* is about the people themselves—their personalities, their stories, their wounds, their questions, their inner scripts.

Read the Room

Both the apostles Paul and Peter could give a master class on contextual communication (a.k.a. reading the room). They always knew who they were talking to. Whether addressing the Jewish legalists in Galatia, the sexually confused in Corinth, or the philosophy lovers in Athens, they tailored their message based on their audience.[1]

One of my mentors used to say that Paul the apostle possessed a unique ability: a rare, Spirit-sharpened insight to connect with and contextualize Christ within any culture he stepped into.

He wasn't just multilingual; he was adept at navigating multiple worldviews. He understood how people thought, what they valued, and what they worshipped. As a Hebrew by birth and a citizen of Rome who was intellectually fluent in Greek philosophy, Paul carried a deep familiarity with three very different worlds (Phil. 3:5; Acts 17:16–34; 22:25–28).

Paul knew that in Jewish culture, the great ideal was light (over darkness); in Greek culture, the chief objective was knowledge; and in Roman culture, the supreme pursuits were glory, honor, triumph, and lasting legacy. It was his intimate knowledge of the ideals in all three cultures that prompted him to write this in his letter to the Corinthian church:

> For God, who said, "Let light shine out of darkness," made His light shine in our hearts to give us the light of the knowledge of the glory of God in the face of Jesus Christ. (2 Cor. 4:6 BSB)

Wait, do you see what Paul did there? He recognized these abstract ideals in each culture and understood that Jesus Himself was the embodiment of them all. In this verse, Christ was the light the Jews longed for, the knowledge the Greeks sought, and the glory the Romans chased.

That's what made Paul so effective. He didn't just preach the gospel; he positioned it. He understood who he was talking to, and because of that, he knew exactly how to contextualize Christ and speak to their hearts.

Another one of Paul's greatest hits was the epic moment on the Areopagus, a location better known among contemporary Christians as Mars Hill. When Paul stood before the intellectual elite of Athens, he didn't quote Scripture. Why? Because they didn't know the Scriptures. Instead, he quoted *their* poets and appealed to their longing for the "unknown god" (Acts 17:22–28 ESV).

That wasn't compromise. It was wisdom. He knew who he was talking to.

Compare that with Peter's audience in Acts 2. He was speaking to devout Jews who already believed in the God of Israel, so Peter didn't need to convince them that God exists. He simply connected the dots between their Scriptures and Jesus as the promised Messiah.

Paul had a unique calling to the Gentiles—people who didn't grow up with the Torah, the Law, or the customs of Israel (Acts 9:15; 13:46–47; Gal. 2:7–9). So when he wrote or spoke to Gentiles, he had to take into account that they weren't familiar with the covenants, the prophets, or the commandments. His letters reflect that. He explained concepts that would have been common knowledge for a Jewish audience, contextualizing them for Gentiles. Peter, on the other hand, primarily addressed Jewish believers, those who were steeped in Old Testament tradition (Gal. 2:7–9), so he spoke and wrote accordingly. In both cases, effectiveness required clarity. A failure to understand their audience would have made Peter and Paul ineffective.

Paul would later write:

> You know how I lived the whole time I was with you.... I served the Lord with great humility and

> with tears.... I have not hesitated to preach anything that would be helpful to you. (Acts 20:18b–20 NIV).

That's the heart of someone who didn't just preach truth but who lived among the people. He learned who they were, then he spoke.

We may not live among people for months or years, but we can spend five minutes asking good questions. We can pause long enough to listen. To locate them. Because when you know where someone is, you can discern whether you're preaching to the choir or reaching to the confused. And that changes everything.

The MAP

Okay, so we've established that reading the room is important. Why? Because people are not carbon copies. They are nuanced. Each person brings a different set of assumptions, values, and experiences into a conversation. Not everyone is starting from the same place. Different people wrestle with truth in different ways. That means we can't afford a copy-and-paste approach.

The questions become: How do we avoid having one-size-fits-all conversations that treat people like carbon copies? And how can we begin to discern who is really sitting across from us in the classroom, coffee shop, or comment section?

Toward better understanding, I developed a blueprint that helps us think of the person across from us as being made up of three invisible layers. Let's call these layers their MAP—their makeup, their angle, and their posture. These three intangibles shape how truth is heard and how connection happens.

Every meaningful conversation needs a MAP. You need to know: who the person is (their makeup), why they think the way they do (their angle), and how they receive ideas (their posture). These layers invisibly shape tone, tension, defensiveness, openness, and the direction of the moment. When you recognize them, you stop reacting only to words and start responding to what's happening in the heart. Following the MAP will prepare you to engage in even the most complicated conversations with clarity, confidence, and compassion.

1. Makeup: Who They Are—Temperament, Wiring, Background

Every person brings a certain posture or worldview orientation into the conversation. Not every unbeliever is the same. Not every critic is hostile. Not every question is an attack. The following four categories help you discern what kind of person you're talking to.

The Seeker

Openhearted and curious. They want to know more, and they're asking real questions without hidden agendas.

The Skeptic

Careful, thoughtful, sometimes wounded. They're not closed—just cautious. Their questions are real but layered with hesitation.

The Cynic

Often shaped by disappointment or betrayal. Their tone is guarded, sarcastic, or combative—but underneath there may be a deeper longing.

The Resolved Unbeliever

They're not seeking—they're settled. They may be vocal, even evangelistic, about their disbelief. Your role here may be less about persuasion and more about planting seeds and staying faithful.

Why This Matters

Understanding their profile shapes how you show up—not to manipulate but to meet them with the tone and timing that match where they actually are.

2. Angle: Why They Think the Way They Do—The Interpretive Lens and the Story That Shaped Their Perspective

This is the inner monologue—the silent, running commentary in someone's mind that interprets your words before they even fully process them. It's the subterranean script shaped by nature, nurture, trauma, upbringing, culture, and conditioning. It's the undercurrent beneath the surface conversation, the pull that directs how they hear and respond.

For example, if a woman has heard her entire life, "All men are dogs," that script shapes how she engages men. He could be a great guy, but she might still assume the worst because she's responding not only to him but to everything she's been conditioned to believe.

Or if someone has always been told, "The church is full of hypocrites," they will often reject your invitation to church—not because of you but because of the inner script already playing in their mind.

They might be smiling on the outside, but inside they're saying:

- *You sound just like the pastor who hurt my family.*
- *You're trying to control me like my parents did.*
- *People like you don't care what happens to people like me.*

You're not just speaking to a person—you're speaking into a story.

Why This Matters

If someone has been spiritually manipulated, even genuine kindness might feel suspicious. If they've seen hypocrisy, truth might sound fake. Knowing their narrative helps you lead with empathy, not evidence.

3. Posture: How They Receive—Openness, Defensiveness, Curiosity

This is about readiness—emotional, spiritual, and intellectual. Are they open, resistant, defensive, distracted? You can't always see it, but it's always influencing the moment.

Jesus paints this picture perfectly in the parable of the sower (Matt. 13:1–23; Mark 4:1–20; Luke 8:4–15).

Each type of soil represents a different kind of heart:

- *Hardened Path:* Truth never gets in. It bounces off—a closed or disinterested heart.
- *Shallow Soil:* Truth is received with excitement but fades quickly. No depth.
- *Thorny Ground:* The message grows but gets choked by worries, riches, and distractions.
- *Good Soil:* Truth is received and understood, and it produces fruit—a heart that's open and ready.

Why This Matters

You could say all the right things—but if the soil isn't ready, the seed won't take root. This isn't a failure of truth. It's a matter of timing, tenderness, and trust.

Clapbacks and Comments

Maybe nowhere is this blueprint more urgently needed, and more frequently ignored, than on social media.

Never has there been a more important place where knowing if someone is a seeker (open and curious), a skeptic (cautious but thoughtful), a cynic (wounded and guarded), or a resolved unbeliever (here to argue, not explore) than on social media.

It's where belief, conscience, expression, and freedom of speech collide every second of every day. In this space, you can find the full spectrum of voices: Pan-Africanists and White supremacists, Muslims and Christians, Republicans and Democrats, progressives and conservatives. It's all there.

And that breadth exists precisely because many of us live in places where speech is free in ways it isn't everywhere. In some parts of the world—think North Korea or Saudi Arabia—public dissent, evangelism, or even unpopular opinions can cost you your job, your freedom ... sometimes your life. By contrast, in the West, we can publish a thought in seconds and reach thousands. That freedom is a gift, and a volatile one. Because with it, people are liable to say anything. They can be offensive, dismissive, sarcastic, hostile, arrogant, patronizing, or flat-out cruel.[2]

I've experienced it firsthand. People have called me a clown, brainwashed, stupid, an idiot, a fairy-tale believer, you name it. And I'm human, so while most of it rolls off, every now and then, someone presses a button. And as tempted as I might be to clap back, I gotta remember who I'm talking to.

Maybe I'm conversing with someone whose inner monologue is riddled with pain, grief, and despair. This person may secretly be a seeker masquerading as a scoffer. Or they could be flat-out disrespectful; I know that's a possibility, as well. But either way, I have a responsibility as a believer to take all the variables into consideration so that even if they are reckless, I know how to maintain composure.

And if I'm honest, that's not always easy. God knows there are moments when I want to snap, clap back, or let my frustration lead the conversation. But taking the full picture into account (who they are, what they may be carrying, and what's at stake) helps me slow down and choose restraint over reaction.

If you struggle in this area too, remember: *The rules don't change because you're online.* Because of the nature of social media and the physical distance between you and the person you're engaging, it's easy to lose sight of the fact that you're still talking to a real human being. The screen creates space. The keyboard creates a buffer. And that distance can subtly convince us that the standards for how we speak, how we engage, and how we treat people have somehow shifted.

But they haven't.

That's why I've had to remind myself of this simple truth: *Typing is talking too.* Just because the conversation is happening through thumbs instead of voices doesn't mean the same principles don't apply. We're still communicating from our hearts. We're still shaping tone. We're still capable of either building bridges or burning them down, one sentence at a time.

It's true: The Bible doesn't explicitly say anything about social media. You won't find a verse about how to post, how to comment, or how to engage on Threads or Instagram.

But this is the brilliance of Jesus. He always went deeper.

Jesus didn't just address actions; He addressed intentions.

He didn't just correct the fruit; He exposed the root.

He didn't just deal with what people did; He confronted why they did it.

When Jesus talked about the things that come out of our mouths, He pointed back to the heart: "Out of the abundance of the heart the mouth speaks" (Matt. 12:34 ESV).

So when I say typing is talking too, I mean this: Just because it didn't come out of your mouth doesn't mean it didn't come out of your heart. Life and death aren't just in the power of the tongue ... they're in the power of the thumbs too.

So yes, the Bible may not mention social media by name, but God's Word does speak to our digital habits today.

Whether you speak it or type it, the biblical principles still apply. "A soft answer turns away wrath" still applies (Prov. 15:1 ESV). "Be quick to hear, slow to speak, slow to anger" still applies (James 1:19 ESV). The tongue is still "a fire" (3:6), and on social media that fire spreads through comment sections. We are still called to "overcome evil with good" (Rom. 12:21). And we are still called to emulate Jesus who, when insulted, "did not retaliate"—He entrusted Himself to the Father (1 Pet. 2:23 NIV). Even when we "give a defense," Scripture requires us to do it "with gentleness and respect, keeping a clear conscience," so that accusers end up ashamed of their slander (3:15–16 BSB).

So no, the internet isn't a loophole. It's a test. The comment section is not an escape from the way of Jesus—it's one of the most practical training grounds for it.

Just because it didn't come out of your mouth doesn't mean it didn't come out of your heart. Life and death aren't just in the power of the tongue ... they're in the power of the thumbs too.

Sometimes that means pausing before you post. Editing yourself. Leading your own heart by speaking words of affirmation before you press Send. I've found that when I thank someone—even a scoffer—for weighing in, it tempers me as much as it tempers the conversation. For example, someone might say something reckless, sideways, or inflammatory, and I'll respond: "Salute, king. Thank you so much for weighing in. I respect your perspective." Then I'll move into my response. I've found that it not only brings the temperature down for them but it also helps me calibrate my own heart before I engage.

I remember one young woman commenting on one of my posts. She gave me props for how I engage people because, she admitted, "the Peter in me wants to come out." We all know what she meant—pulling the sword, swinging wildly, cutting off ears. We laughed, and I told her: "Peter is in me too. But I choose to take the high road—to be more like Christ. That's not easy. That's a conscious choice to bless those who curse me online." *And because that choice isn't always natural, I've learned I need to pray before I post.* It's the way I keep my heart aligned before I move my thumbs.

Pray Before You Post

While I think it's important to pause before you post, I've also discovered something equally imperative: *praying before you pos*t. This has been a game changer for me. Over this past year, I've found that it's not the pause that helps—it's the prayer.

This isn't a rule. It's not a mandate. I'm not saying everyone must do it. But for me, it's become a deeply beneficial rhythm.

I've seen how quickly online conversations can spiral, and how unprepared my heart can be if I rush into them. Prayer slows me down long enough to check my ego, soften my posture, and anchor me in the Spirit before I enter a thread where anything can happen. It helps me respond to people instead of provocation. It positions me to approach digital engagement with *pure intention*, *prepared posture*, and *peaceful engagement*—three things I desperately need before I engage.

And honestly, this habit has shaped not just my spirit but my tone. It gives me room to step into tension with clarity instead of combativeness, with compassion instead of pride.

Realistically, not every exchange will end with agreement. Some cynics will stay cynical. Some resolved unbelievers will never budge. But I've seen how the tone of my response can change the tone of an entire thread. A cynical person who mocks your faith may soften when you answer with respect. A resolved unbeliever who dismisses Christianity as a myth may at least pause when you affirm their humanity before making your case.

At the end of the day, understanding someone's profile helps you meet them where they are. Paying attention to their narrative helps you speak with empathy instead of ego. And recognizing their disposition helps you sow wisely instead of wastefully. Remember, the goal isn't to be right—it's to reflect Jesus rightly. That's what makes every interaction sacred. Every question, every objection, every dialogue becomes an opportunity, not simply to prove a point but to reveal a Person.

CURIOUS CONVERSATION

What do we do with spiritual experiences outside of Christianity?

As I mentioned before, Paul the apostle once found himself on a hill in Athens, standing among philosophers, thinkers, and deeply spiritual people (Acts 17:22–34). The Greeks were polytheists, so the city was filled with altars to various gods. But one altar in particular stood out. It was marked: "To the unknown god" (v. 23 ESV). They had made room for mystery—for the possibility that there was a god they hadn't yet discovered.

Paul had been invited to speak because word had spread about his message. And what he did in that moment is something we can learn from: He didn't start by condemning their worldview. He started by affirming their God-consciousness, their spiritual hunger, and their search for meaning. But he didn't stop there. He used their altar to the unknown god as an opportunity to point them toward the true and living God.

That moment reminds me of a question (or more accurately, a challenge) I hear often in conversations about faith. Let's zero in on that conversation.

Possible Dialogue

Them—Objection

People had sacred, meaningful spiritual experiences for thousands of years before Jesus ever showed up. What did they do before Him? Are you saying all those gods weren't real? Isn't it arrogant to dismiss everything that came before Christianity?

You—Rude Response

Because they were wrong. There's only one God, and every other god was fake.

Why This Doesn't Work

It shuts down conversation instead of opening it. It dismisses, oversimplifies, and ignores the fact that spiritual experiences differ in source, purpose, and reliability. Scripture offers categories for spiritual experiences that are real but also limited, incomplete, misdirected, or costly. Below, I outline them in contemporary language.

Better Response

You—Affirmation

I actually think that's a really important question, especially because it raises issues about fairness and about not boxing God in. And honestly, if Jesus is the only way, it's natural to wonder what that means for our ancestors who lived long before the Incarnation.

Empathy

I get that. I've wrestled with it myself over the years. It's a valid question, and you're not the first person to ask it.

Ask

Do you feel like the claim that there's "one truth" sounds unfair or too exclusive—maybe even like Christians are trying to dominate the narrative in a way that feels like colonialism or imperialism?

Answer

This is a layered question, so I want to respond to it in a couple different ways. First, as it pertains to what people did before Jesus: Christianity is late, but Christ is not.

People often assume that Jesus' arrival is the same as His existence—that He came into being when He was born in Bethlehem. In other words, the assumption is that Jesus began to exist in the first century. But that's not the Christian claim, and it never has been (John 1:1–2; Phil. 2:6–7).

According to Scripture, Jesus didn't come into existence at His birth. That's only when He entered physical history. The Incarnation marks a moment in time, not the beginning of His being. While Christ did enter history in a unique and decisive way in the first century, He was not created then. Christianity as an organized movement or recognizable religion may have taken shape during that period, but *the Christ of Christianity did not begin there* (John 8:58; Col. 1:17).

Not only has Christ always existed but the Bible goes even further by identifying Him as the very agent of creation itself (John 1:3; Col. 1:16; Heb. 1:2).

Which means we may actually be asking the wrong question. The question isn't "What were people supposed to do before Jesus existed?" Because biblically speaking, *Jesus didn't begin to exist in the first century*. The eternal Christ, the One through whom all things were made, has been present from the very beginning (Rev. 22:13; 1 Cor. 10:4). That reframes the entire conversation.

This isn't simply about when Christianity started as a religion; it's about *who people were encountering and responding to throughout human history*. From the Christian perspective, it has been Christ all along, revealing Himself in different ways to different people across different moments in time.

So although I understand what people mean when they ask what people did "before Jesus," that question is categorically incorrect. Technically, there is no time before Jesus, so the idea that Jesus is a late addition doesn't hold. Humanity wasn't waiting on God to show up for salvation. He was already present, and He has been doing His work since the beginning, as salvation has always been through Christ.

Different methods of revelation (Rev. 1:1–2). Same object of salvation.

Possible Dialogue

Them—Rebuttal 1

Okay, but what about spiritual experiences in other cultures?

You—Rude Response

Those experiences were demonic. Period.

Why This Doesn't Work

It oversimplifies complex spiritual realities and ignores Scripture's nuance. Not all supernatural experiences come from the same source. Not all are evil. Some are limited, some incomplete, some misdirected, some costly. A dismissive answer blocks understanding.

Better Response

You—Affirm

I'm not here to invalidate spiritual experiences. I don't doubt that what is encountered is real and meaningful.

Empathize

I understand how deeply these moments can shape a person. Some experiences stay with us for years because they felt sacred or transcendent.

Ask

Would you mind if I shared with you a few different ways that might help you make sense of what you experienced?

Answer

Here are a few categories Scripture gives us:

1. Real ... but Limited

Pharaoh's magicians produced real supernatural signs (Ex. 7–8). They had power, but it was finite, they could only go so far before being forced to admit that the God whom Moses served produced signs from "the finger of God" (8:19). Some experiences are real but limited.

2. Supernatural ... but Not Saving

Some experiences are spiritual but do not reconcile us to God nor reveal the gospel. Scripture says, "Even Satan disguises himself as an angel of light" (2 Cor. 11:14 ESV). The tension is that it's easy to confuse a powerful supernatural experience with spiritual transformation. But those two are not synonymous.

3. Impactful ... but Incomplete

Cornelius prayed, gave generously, and lived uprightly (Acts 10). God noticed it, maybe even honored it in some way. But his deepest need remained unmet. Not because his goodness was false but because it was still incomplete. Cornelius still needed Christ for salvation.

4. Mystical ... but Misdirected and Marginal

Simon the sorcerer possessed real supernatural influence. His practices were persuasive, impressive, and those who followed him even described his power as "great." But his power was self-referential—it drew attention to himself rather than pointing to the authority of Christ. When measured against the actual power of God, it was exposed as insufficient and ultimately hollow (Acts 8:9–24).

The presence of spiritual power that is detached from Christ may feel transcendent, but it stops short of the source, whose power is greater.

5. Convenient ... but Costly

Some spiritual practices offer quick results or emotional highs but leave spiritual residue, confusion, bondage, or fragmentation. "The blessing of the LORD makes one rich, and He adds no sorrow with it" (Prov. 10:22). Counterfeit spirituality often adds sorrow.

Possible Dialogue

Them—Rebuttal 2

I still don't see why there has to be only one God.

You—Rude Response

Because the Bible says so, and that's that. It is what it is.

Why This Doesn't Work

It dismisses the emotional weight behind the statement, ignores the historical struggle of polytheistic cultures, and bypasses the biblical pattern of discerning truth through testing.

Better Response

You—Affirm

I understand why the idea of "one true God" can feel restrictive at first.

Empathize

Wanting spiritual freedom makes sense. We live in a world of endless options. I get why that matters.

Ask

Why do you think the idea of one true God feels restrictive? Does it feel like it limits your spiritual agency?

Answer

We live in a culture overloaded with choices for our clothes, shows, and apps. After a while, we grow weary of so many options and burn out. Psychologists and sociologists call this decision fatigue.[3] So for me, the idea of one God isn't limiting—it's clarifying.

But this isn't new. The struggle with "one God versus many gods" is not a modern dilemma. The ancient world was overwhelmingly polytheistic. People wrestled with these same questions: Which god is the true God? Is there only one? (See 1 Kings 18:21.)

The good thing is that we are not left without a way to find an answer. There *is* a way to discern truth. There *was* a way ancient people used to discover which god was real. And that way was through *testing*. Let me show you what I mean.

Take the case of King Nebuchadnezzar, for example (Dan. 2:1–47). He believed in many gods. When he had a disturbing dream, he summoned every spiritual expert he had: magicians, sorcerers, astrologers, wise men. They all claimed access to the divine. They all claimed supernatural insight. But none of them could tell him the dream *or* its interpretation. Then Daniel, serving the God of Israel, stepped forward. In one moment, God revealed both the dream and its meaning—something no other "god" could do.

What do we discover from this story? That many gods were worshipped. Many claimed power. But only one God answered.

Nebuchadnezzar acknowledged it: "Truly your God is the God of gods, the Lord of kings" (v. 47).

We also see this in Elijah's showdown with the false god Baal (1 Kings 18:16–39). Israel was divided between worshipping Yahweh and Baal, so Elijah proposed a public test: "The God who answers by fire, He is God" (v. 24). The prophets of Baal cried out from morning to evening. They danced. They shouted. They cut themselves. They tried everything to get Baal to send fire. *Silence*. Then Elijah prayed a simple prayer, and fire fell immediately.

What do we discover? That neither sincerity nor devotion is the measure of truth. *Response* is the measure. The living God answers. He is the God who saves.

In both of these scenarios, the culture had many gods. The options were overwhelming. The spiritual landscape was crowded. Yet there was still a way to discern the truth.

The real questions become: Which God answers? Which God speaks? Which God reveals? Which God interprets reality? Which God explains the human condition? Which God knows who we are and why we're here? Which God addresses the deepest longings of the soul—purpose, identity, meaning, morality, destiny, eternity?

And historically, the answer is consistent: *The God of the Bible answered. The others did not.*

So if someone genuinely wants to know whether there is a true God, they don't have to guess. Ask the question that ancient people asked: Which God answers? God Himself invites this. "Put me to the test" (see Mal. 3:10 ESV).

To be clear, this is not a promise that God will meet every expectation, heal every sickness, or resolve every circumstance on our terms. Scripture never presents God as obligated to perform on demand. What it does promise, clearly and without qualification, is that "everyone who calls on the name of the Lord will be saved" (Rom. 10:13 NIV). This is the one assurance Scripture guarantees, not because God has been proven to exist but because He has made Himself known. In that sense, faith does not force God's hand; it responds to His promise.

You don't have to blindly accept anything. If you want to know the truth—*test Him*.

KEYS FOR THE CONVERSATION

Every chapter has a lot of moving pieces, but if you can remember these keys, you'll carry the heart of this chapter and the tools you'll need into every conversation.

1. What You Need to Know

People are not one-size-fits-all.

Every person brings their own worldview, wounds, personality, assumptions, and history into a conversation. Two people can say the exact same words and mean completely different things because they're shaped by different stories.

Understanding *who is in front of you* increases the likelihood of an effective, meaningful conversation.

2. What You Need to Do

Identify the layers within the person.

Pay attention to their *profile* (seeker, skeptic, cynic, resolved unbeliever), their *disposition* (open or closed), and their *narrative* (the story shaping how they hear you). The clearer the picture, the better you can engage.

3. Who You Need to Become

Become someone patient enough to slow down, ask good questions, and genuinely discover the person in front of you. Become someone disciplined enough to resist the temptation to "copy and paste" answers and committed enough to tailor your approach, because every person is different.

Chapter 3

RIDESHARE: THE POWER OF A RELATABLE STORY

Your story could be the key that unlocks someone else's prison.

Unknown

The engine hummed as the city blurred past our windows. We were about ten minutes into an Uber ride when the driver asked what I do for a living, and, like it usually does when that happens, the conversation opened up.

She told me she used to go to church but now struggled to go or even to believe in God, ever since her fifteen-year-old nephew—who was on a good track in life, wasn't on the streets, and had no known enemies—was shot and killed. The murder of her loved one had shaken her to the core.

Naturally, I did what I usually do when that kind of statement hits the air: I tried to help.

First, I tried to appeal to her heart, talking about the compassion of God, how He hurts when we hurt, how He's not indifferent to our pain.

That didn't work.

Then I tried to create some distance between the crime and the character of God. I told her that what happened to her family wasn't God's doing, that He's good even when the world isn't.

That didn't work either.

So I pivoted again. I talked about how God gives humans free will, how we're capable of both beauty and destruction, and how sometimes the pain we experience is the result of broken people making broken choices.

But even that didn't seem to connect.

Each time I spoke, she nodded politely, but I could tell she wasn't moved. She was listening, but we weren't connecting. My words were true, but they weren't helping. It felt like the answers were hitting her mind but missing her heart.

I could feel the opportunity slipping away. I had tried three or four different angles, and nothing was landing. So I took a breath. There were about ten minutes left in the ride, and I thought, *Maybe I've done all I can.*

But then, in a quiet moment, I decided to try one last thing. Instead of offering another explanation or one of those familiar rebuttals we tend to pull out, I reached for something else: a story.

"Have you ever heard of a man named Job?" I asked.

She shook her head.

So I began to tell her about Job, a man who was faithful to God yet endured unimaginable loss. Job's children were killed, his wealth was destroyed, his health was taken, and he was left sitting in ashes asking the same question she was asking: Why?

I told her about Job's friends, how they came to comfort him but instead ended up making things worse with their shallow explanations and mistaken theology (Job 2:11–13; 16:2). And I told her about Job's wife, who, broken by grief herself, told him to "curse God and die" (2:9), demonstrating how even those closest to him couldn't understand the depth of his pain. Yet in all of it, Job never stopped being honest with God (3; 6:24; 13:3).

Then I told her about the moment when God finally spoke to Job, not to answer every question, but to reveal His wisdom and His presence in a way that changed everything (38–42).

As I spoke, I could feel the energy in the car shift. She wasn't just listening. She was leaning in.

By the time I finished, she looked over at me and said something I didn't expect: "I think I'm going to go to church this Sunday."

But why? Why the shift all of a sudden? We had been talking for nearly thirty minutes by that point. What had caused everything to change?

It was the power of a story.

The story of Job did what all my arguments could not: It reached her in the deepest recesses of her soul.

Why Stories Work

Looking back, that ride reminded me why stories matter so much.

I tried reason, theology, and empathy ... all good things, for sure. But none of them connected. It wasn't until I shared a *story* that the conversation shifted from comprehension to connection.

I'm a huge fan of comedian Dave Chappelle, not only because of his humor but because of his storytelling. His social commentary is sharp, but it's his ability to take you on a journey, to make you laugh, think, and feel, that makes his art unforgettable. He pulls you in and disarms you with the power of narrative.

Stories are universal. They meet people where they are—in their pain, their questions, their humanity. They create a safe space for reflection and offer a way to see a bigger picture without being forceful.

Stories build bridges. Whether it's your personal story or, as in the case of that young woman, that of someone else, stories help form inroads and establish common ground.

And this is why Jesus employed stories: He understood their power. He used parables not only to teach but to test hearts.

In some sense, Jesus' parables carry theological mystery. When His disciples asked why He spoke to the crowds in parables, He told them that the hidden meaning of His stories wasn't for everyone. Some would hear but never understand. Some would see but never truly perceive. It wasn't to hide truth from those who genuinely sought it—but to expose the blindness of those who refused to (Mark 4:11–12).

Yet while His parables revealed the condition of hearts, they also built bridges.

Interestingly enough, we tend to think that Jesus came up with every parable and story He told. But there are several instances where He likely drew from stories circulating in the culture, familiar frameworks His listeners already knew. He leveraged those narratives, reframed them, and used them as connecting points to reveal divine truth and as an entry point into what they didn't yet understand.

I know this idea may come as a surprise. I get it. It can feel jarring at first to imagine Jesus drawing from stories that were already mainstream. You might even wonder if it diminishes His originality or authority. But it doesn't—not at all. In fact, it highlights something beautiful.

Jesus wasn't copying; He was *connecting.* He was stepping into a long-standing Jewish storytelling tradition known as the *mashal,* a broad category that includes parables, proverbs, riddles, similes, allegories, and short narrative stories used for instruction. As scholar Klyne Snodgrass points out, Jesus didn't invent the genre. Rather, He stepped into the mashal tradition that Israel had been using for centuries, and He elevated it, sharpened it, and filled it with kingdom meaning.[1]

We actually see mashal-style storytelling long before Jesus. Think of the prophet Nathan confronting David with the story of the poor man's lamb (2 Sam. 12). That was a mashal, a narrative crafted to reveal the heart and expose truth. Other Jewish teachers, sages, and rabbis used similar story forms. It was part of the culture's way of thinking, teaching, and processing truth.

And many of the motifs Jesus used—the vineyard, the father and sons, the king's banquet, the wedding feast, tenant imagery—were familiar elements within that tradition. His listeners already had categories for these images. So Jesus wasn't diminishing His message by drawing on known story patterns. *He was making it more accessible.* He was building bridges with imagery His audience already understood so He could lead them somewhere deeper.

And that's the beauty of it: Jesus used familiar forms to communicate unfamiliar truths. He took what they knew and used it to reveal what they didn't know.

This reminds us that stories don't just teach; they *reveal.* They uncover the posture of a person's heart toward truth. And that's why, to this day, storytelling holds power.

My Story

When I was growing up in church, particularly in the Baptist tradition, there used to be a thing called testimony service. It happened maybe once a month, and people would stand up and share stories of what God had done in their lives.

I'd hear people tell these radical, cinematic stories of deliverance: God saving them from drugs, prison, violence, prostitution, and every kind of chaos you could imagine. Their testimonies were the stuff of movies.

Mine? Well, not so much.

I came to faith at the tender age of five. I grew up in a Christian home. My parents were pastors and teachers, and my sisters sang on the praise and worship team at my father's church. I went to Hallelujah Night (our alternative to Halloween), Friday night Bible study, all-night prayer meetings, and Sunday morning services, and on Halloween, I dressed up in sheets as Lazarus. Fun for me was when all the sister churches got together and the youth ministries from those churches met up. That was a big deal back then—a kind of holy "youth bash."

So, as you can imagine, sitting in testimony service, comparing my stories with the others, mine felt inferior. In fact, I used to sit in those testimony services thinking, *Man ... if that's what a testimony is, maybe I don't have one.*

But then I realized my testimony was not that God had dragged me out of the mud but rather that He had "kept me." And that realization became such a part of me that I eventually wrote a song about it called "My Story."

The chorus goes:

> I ain't got no horror story,
> God kept me in my youth.
> I gave Him all the glory,
> thought my story wouldn't float.
> But now I know the blood of the Lamb saved my soul—
> and that's my testimony.[2]

That song became a kind of anthem for me and for a lot of church kids who grew up feeling like their story wasn't "dramatic" enough. It reminded us that God doesn't just rescue from the pit; He also keeps us from falling into it.

God doesn't just rescue from the pit; He also keeps us from falling into it.

The heart of God is to preserve His people. In fact, I'm convinced that He would rather preserve us than have to restore us.

That was my soapbox for years ... until more life happened, and I made poor choices and experienced moral failures and lapses in judgment that caused real pain to others and myself. There are moments I wish I could erase, and there are consequences I still carry.

My story is now a hybrid one, the tale of many seasons. It's a story of both preservation and restoration.

Because God has a way of taking the muted tones along with the bright colors, both the major keys and minor keys, and weaving them all together into something unexpectedly beautiful.

The Power of the Bible's Stories and Sacred Scandal

There's power not only in our personal stories but also in the stories of others.

As in the case of the Uber driver, sometimes the story that changes someone's heart isn't our own.

In that moment, it wasn't my words or explanations that reached her. It was Job's story, one that gave language to her pain and showed her that God can still be present even when life feels cruel.

This is what the Bible does so beautifully. It's a book full of individual stories that exist within the broader context of a single, unfolding narrative, what theologians call the metanarrative of Scripture.

From the wonder of creation to the corruption of the fall, from the redemption accomplished through Christ to the ultimate restoration of all things, the Bible tells one grand story—the story of God's relentless pursuit of humanity.

But as beautiful as the grand story is, the stories in between are scandalous.

They are not sanitized. In fact, the Bible is messy. It's bloody. It's raw and unfiltered, filled with the tension of humanity and the holiness of God colliding in real time.

It's the rise and fall of nations. The betrayal of brothers. The lies of prophets. The pride of kings. The chaos of war and the corruption of power (Gen. 37; 2 Sam. 11; 1 Kings 16:30).

It reads less like a tidy religious text and more like something straight out of *Game of Thrones*—full of intrigue, deception, and drama, yet threaded with divine redemption.

Within its pages are men and women who fail miserably, leaders who abuse power, families that are torn apart, and nations that self-destruct.

There are wars, murders, moral failures, and acts so disturbing that many people today struggle to reconcile them with the idea of a loving God (Judg. 2:11–12 and chapters 19–21).

And that's exactly the pushback we often hear.

Modern thinkers, critics, and cultural commentators, from talk-show hosts to podcast philosophers, read parts of the Bible and recoil. They see the violence, the deceit, the genocide, the corruption and say, "If this is the Word of God, how can He possibly be good?"

Some—including thought leaders such as Bill Maher, a comedian and social commentator known for his sharp wit and unapologetic atheism—have expressed open disgust at what has been called "the barbarism of the Bible."

To them, the gore, bloodshed, and moral failures disqualify the Scriptures from being divine.

But I see it differently. What they see as evidence against the Bible, I see as evidence *for* it. What they see as scandal, I see as unsanitized stories that both bear witness and build bridges. These same stories bear witness to the problem God has been describing all along.

They testify that the world is broken, that sin is real, that depravity is not a theory but a lived reality. Every lie, every act of violence, every ounce of corruption is not a contradiction of God's Word but a confirmation of it.

The Bible doesn't just diagnose the problem; it explains its root. The chaos we see in its pages mirrors the chaos we see in our world today, both flowing from the same place: the human heart.

The Bible's stories also build bridges because they connect us across centuries.

When we read about betrayal, lust, greed, jealousy, and pain, we recognize ourselves in the text. We see our own reflection in the lives of Abraham, Eve, Jacob, Rahab, David, Mary, and Peter. These stories remind us that human nature hasn't changed and that God's grace still reaches for us right where we are.

So while critics call these stories disturbing, I see them as deeply honest. They don't hide from the tension ... they expose it. And in doing so, they prove that God has properly diagnosed the sickness of humanity and, through the same narrative, revealed the cure.

The very thing that offends modern sensibilities is what confirms the Bible's authenticity.

If the Scriptures were fiction or propaganda for a perfect religion, the writers would've scrubbed the shameful details, edited out the ugly parts, and polished the people into saints. But they didn't.

The Bible tells the truth about the human condition, and it tells it without filters. It records:

- Abraham lying out of fear (Gen. 12:10–20; 20:1–18).
- Jacob deceiving his father (Gen. 27:1–29).
- Moses killing a man in anger (Exod. 2:11–12).

- David committing adultery and orchestrating murder (2 Sam. 11:1–27).
- Peter denying Jesus (Matt. 26:69–75).
- Saul persecuting the church (Acts 8:1–3; 9:1–2).

It doesn't glorify their sin, but it doesn't hide it either. Because God isn't afraid of the truth—He redeems it. And that's what makes the Scriptures powerful. They don't just show us who the biblical characters were; they show us who *we are*. Every character, every story, every failure, and every triumph becomes a mirror reflecting our own humanity back to us—and a window revealing a God who meets us in the middle of it.

The stories of the Bible are biography and bridge. They reveal the human story, and they connect us to the divine one.

At the end of the day, that's what all this is about—story.

Whether it's a stranger's heartbreak in an Uber, my own winding journey of preservation and redemption, or the scandalous honesty of Scripture, God has always chosen story as His vehicle of truth.

So tell your story.

Tell it with humility.

Tell it with honesty.

Tell it knowing that somewhere, someone is sitting in their own version of that Uber ride—waiting for a story that gives language to their pain.

Because the story of God is still unfolding, and He's chosen us to help tell it in order to point people back to Him.

CURIOUS CONVERSATION

"Why does a good God allow so many bad things and suffering?"

Possible Dialogue

Them—Objection

I hear people say that God is good—but if He is so good, why does He allow so much evil and suffering ... not just in the world, but in my own life?

You—Rude Response

I don't know. Ask Him. Maybe He can tell you.

Why This Doesn't Work

Sarcasm might feel like a quick defense mechanism, but it shuts down honest dialogue. Most people who ask this aren't posing a philosophical riddle—they're carrying something personal, painful, and unresolved. What they need is compassion, not cleverness.

Better Response

You—Affirm

You're absolutely right to ask that question. When you look at the pain in this world—the suffering, the injustice, the inequity, the things people go through that shake you to your core—it would almost be strange *not* to ask it. Life hits hard. And when it does, the question, "If God is good, why would He allow this?" becomes not only understandable ... it becomes necessary.

Empathize

And I get it. I've been through seasons so heavy that I asked God the very same thing. I've wrestled with doubts—not just about His existence but about His character. His goodness. His fairness. His nearness. I've had moments when I didn't understand what He was doing and, honestly, moments when I didn't understand Him at all. So you're not alone in asking. I've been there too.

Ask

What does the hardship of life make you think about God? When you think about what you've been through—or what you've seen others endure—what comes to your mind about Him? What other thoughts rise to the surface for you?

Answer

Here's the truth: God allows evil because He refuses to violate the very thing that makes us human—our will (Deut. 30:19; Josh. 24:15). Human freedom is a gift, but it's also a tremendous risk. The moment God chose to give people genuine agency, He accepted the reality that we would use that freedom in very different ways (Gen. 2:16–17).

On the upside, that freedom is what allows for love, loyalty, compassion, creativity, justice, mercy, and every act of goodness we celebrate. Human beings build hospitals, rescue strangers, fight for justice, adopt children, serve the vulnerable, and sacrificially love one another—all because we are free (Mic. 6:8; Gal. 5:13–14).

But the downside is equally real: With that same freedom, people choose to harm, deceive, betray, abuse, oppress, and destroy (Jer. 17:9; Rom. 3:10–18). Human agency has a dark edge, and the painful truth is that God's commitment to giving us real choice means He must also allow us to live with the consequences of those choices (Gal. 6:7–8).

Still, He honors our will because anything less would make us something other than human. If God controlled every decision we made, our actions wouldn't be ours at all. If He prevented every harmful choice, then love wouldn't be genuine, obedience wouldn't be authentic, and morality wouldn't be meaningful (1 John 4:19; Rom. 6:16). We would be no different from animals driven by instinct or artificial intelligence running programming scripts.

So yes—human freedom carries a cost. It allows for astonishing beauty and heartbreaking evil. That's the unavoidable tension of a world where agency is real (Eccl. 7:29).

But this leads to the real question: Is God responsible for the evil that people commit with the freedom He gave them?

The answer is no.

Because the evil deeds people commit flow from their own hearts, not His (Mark 7:21–23; James 1:13–15). God allows freedom, but He is not the author of the decisions made with that freedom. He grants agency, but He doesn't plant the malice, cruelty, or rebellion that fuels human wrongdoing. The darkness in the world does not originate in Him—it originates in us (Gen. 6:5; Rom. 1:24–28).

In other words:

God is responsible for giving freedom.

People are responsible for how they use it.

Freedom explains why evil is possible, but it does not make God the source of evil (James 1:17).

Possible Dialogue

Them—Rebuttal 1

Okay, I guess that sort of makes sense, but I've heard pastors say human suffering is actually a blessing. Some even claim slavery or the Holocaust were "used for good." That's offensive to me.

You—Rude Response

Well, God uses everything for His glory, so ...

Why This Doesn't Work

Because it's not just insensitive—it's harmful. It suggests God endorses evil to accomplish good, which misrepresents His character and wounds people who are already hurting.

Better Response

You—Affirm

I know. I've heard that too—and those statements aren't just problematic; they're deeply offensive. They come from a place that is at best ignorant and, at worst, profoundly dark and wicked.

Empathize

I once heard a pastor say slavery was a blessing because "it brought Black people to America." Hearing that broke something in me. Statements like that distort God's character and retraumatize people who are already carrying generational pain.

Ask

When you hear statements like that about God and suffering, what does it make you think about His character? Does it make Him feel harsh, distant, or indifferent?

Answer

Let me start by saying that this perspective is not just insensitive; it is morally disturbing. No matter who says it or what platform they have, it is unbiblical to suggest that slavery and the Holocaust were somehow "blessings in disguise." It paints a picture of God that is nothing like the God revealed in Scripture.

If you believe God orchestrates atrocities to accomplish good, then you end up with a deity who is indifferent to—and a promoter of—human suffering, complicit in oppression, and comfortable with injustice. That is not the God of the Bible.

The overwhelming witness of Scripture is that God is good, righteous, compassionate, and just (Ps. 145:17; 34:8; Nah. 1:7). And genuine righteousness can't stay neutral in the face of evil. Righteousness must oppose whatever contradicts it. That means:

- God hates oppression (Ps. 103:6; Isa. 1:17).
- He hates injustice (Ps. 11:7; Deut. 32:4).

- He hates violence (Ps. 11:5).
- He hates the shedding of innocent blood (Prov. 6:16–17).
- He grieves with the brokenhearted (Ps. 34:18).
- He comforts those who mourn (Isa. 61:1–3).
- He draws near to the crushed in spirit (Ps. 34:18).

And while some people use verses like Isaiah 45:7 ("I … create disaster" NIV) or references to Job's suffering to argue that God orchestrates pain, the full weight of Scripture leans in the exact opposite direction. Scripture says that every good and perfect gift comes from Him (James 1:17). Jesus teaches that He loves giving good gifts to His children (Matt. 7:11). David declares that God's goodness and mercy follow us all the days of our lives (Ps. 23:6).

God is not the architect of slavery, genocide, murder, abuse, or terror. Human sin, not God, is responsible for those things (Gen. 6:5; Rom. 3:23; Jer. 17:9). To suggest that God "used" slavery or the Holocaust as blessings is not only a gross misreading of Scripture, it's a severe distortion of His character. God does not need evil to do good. He is powerful enough to bring about good *in spite of* evil, never *through* the evil itself (Gen. 50:20; Rom. 8:28).

The evil acts of human beings reveal the darkness of the human heart—not the nature of God's heart (Mark 7:20–23; James 1:13–15).

One more thing that's important to understand: God is not only compassionate toward the oppressed—He is their defender (Ps. 68:5; 9:9–10; Deut. 10:18). Scripture consistently reveals a God who *vindicates* those who have suffered at the hands of wicked people (Isa. 35:4;

Luke 18:7–8). Every oppressor will face divine accountability. God is a righteous judge, and justice will be served—if not in this life, then in the next (Heb. 9:27; Rev. 20:11–15).

And this matters. *Just because judgment is not immediate does not mean it isn't coming* (Eccl. 8:11).

This is why humans do not have to take vengeance into their own hands. Scripture says, "Vengeance is Mine, I will repay" (Rom. 12:19). And the reason we can trust that is because His judgment is perfect, His justice is pure, and His character is unchanging. He sees every wound, every injustice, every sorrow—and He will make all things right.

Them—Rebuttal 2

Okay, I hear you, but I'm still a little skeptical. With everything that we go through, sometimes I wonder if God really cares.

You—Affirm

You stand in a long line of people in Scripture who have asked the same thing. God isn't offended by your question—He can handle it.

Empathize

With all the suffering and evil in the world, trust me, you're not alone in wondering.

Ask

Would it bring you comfort to know that He truly does care? That He's not indifferent to our pain?

Answer

I understand the place your question comes from. Life hits hard, and when it does, it's natural to wonder, *Does God really care?* The truth is, anyone can tell you they care. Other faiths can offer ideas of peace, compassion, or divine concern. But the problem is, those are just claims, words, concepts, ideals.

But Christianity is different. In Christianity, God doesn't just *say* He cares. He doesn't just talk a good game. *He proves it.* The life of Jesus is the *embodiment* of God's compassion, God's nearness, and God's heart toward us. In Him, God steps into our story. God becomes visible. God becomes touchable.

So in Jesus, we don't merely have vague theories about God's empathy, we have a Person whose entire life is the evidence.

He felt the full weight of the brokenness we experience. He knew grief. He knew physical and emotional pain. He knew betrayal and accusation. He knew rejection. He knew death. And from the cross He cried, "My God, My God, why have You forsaken Me?" (Matt. 27:46).

That is not the cry of a distant deity. That is the cry of a God who suffers *for us and with us.*

Long before Jesus came, the prophets pointed toward One who would be rejected, misunderstood, mistreated, and deeply wounded—not a God far off, but a God who would fully enter human suffering (Isa. 53). Jesus fulfills that promise.

But it isn't only that He suffered—*He felt the suffering of others.*

When He saw Mary weeping over Lazarus, Jesus wept too (John 11:33, 35). Her grief moved Him. Her pain became His pain.

This is why Christianity can answer the question "Does God care?" in a way no other worldview can. It doesn't give you a concept. It gives you a *Person*—a God who steps into your world, carries your sorrows, feels your wounds, and refuses to leave you alone in them.

Them—Rebuttal 3

Okay, well, this might be a little different, but what about natural disasters? Why would God allow those?

You—Affirm

That's a great question. I wish we didn't have to deal with earthquakes, tornadoes, hurricanes, mudslides, or tsunamis. They feel completely outside our control.

Empathize

I've never personally lived through one, but I've seen the devastation—and the grief is overwhelming.

Ask

Have you or someone you love ever been affected by a natural disaster? What did it make you feel or think about God?

Answer

Not only do human beings long for things to be made right, but creation itself also longs for restoration. The Bible teaches this clearly.

Paul says that all creation "groans," waiting, aching, and straining for renewal (Rom. 8:22). The world is broken, and like us, it longs to be healed.

Earthquakes, hurricanes, tornadoes, mudslides, ice storms—none of these were ever part of God's original design. In the beginning, creation was ordered, stable, harmonious, and good. But unfortunately, all of creation was corrupted when sin entered the world. The Bible describes the reason for this disruption, decay, and instability as the ripple effect of human rebellion in Genesis.

Still, that groaning won't last forever.

Scripture promises a day when creation itself will be restored—renewed, redeemed, and brought back into perfect harmony under God's rule. The earthquakes, the storms, the decay, the instability we see now are signs of a world that is not yet what it will be. The same God who restores people will one day restore the cosmos. The brokenness is temporary. The renewal is certain.

KEYS FOR THE CONVERSATION

Every chapter has a lot of moving pieces, but if you can remember these keys, you'll carry the heart of this chapter and the tools you'll need into every conversation.

1. What You Need to Know

Stories disarm people in ways arguments never can. A personal story lowers defenses, builds connection, and creates a bridge between someone's world and yours.

2. What You Need to Do

Use story as your on-ramp. Instead of leading with claims, start with something human—a moment, an experience, a tension, or a lesson you learned.

3. Who You Need to Become

Become the kind of person who sees the moments of your own life—your failures, your doubts, your breakthroughs—as ministry tools. Be someone unafraid to be vulnerable and human. Be intentional about using your story not to spotlight yourself but to guide people toward Jesus.

Chapter 4

BODY LANGUAGE

The most important thing in communication is hearing what isn't said.

Peter Drucker

When you're a kid, few things are as terrifying as the stern stare of your mother—especially when you're caught red-handed. Many of us know what it's like to feel that intense, fiery gaze from across the room. Without saying a word, our mothers could stop us in our tracks. That's the undeniable power of body language. It is the ability to say everything you need to say without ever speaking a word.

One cold and rainy day in London, I was reminded of just how impactful body language is. While walking through Leicester Square, I passed a group of Muslim men handing out pamphlets and engaging people in conversations about their faith. I hadn't planned on stopping. I was cold and eager to reach my destination. But one of them approached me and started a conversation.

At first, it was just him and me, and as we went back and forth, I raised questions about Muhammad and the Qur'an. There was a moment where he seemed stuck, as if he didn't have a response. That's when he went to get their leader, the "chief apologist," to continue the exchange with me. And it was in that conversation with the leader where body language suddenly became the issue.

As we debated, I occasionally placed a hand on his shoulder or chuckled as I made a point. To me, it felt like spirited banter, two people jousting with ideas. But midway through, I noticed he seemed unsettled. Finally, he looked at me and asked, "Why do you keep touching me and laughing every time you make a point?"

I was stunned. I hadn't realized my gestures were bothering him. I initially felt defensive. I hadn't meant to offend. But I knew an apology was in order. For the next several minutes, I tried to explain my intentions, but eventually, remembering that intent doesn't negate impact, I simply said, "I'm sorry."

The truth is, I had no idea what his relationship with touch was. I didn't know if physical contact made him uncomfortable, if he had personal boundaries regarding touch, if there were religious or cultural implications in play, or if past experiences had a role in his reaction. I also didn't know how he viewed interactions with men specifically when it came to physical gestures. To some, his response might seem overly sensitive, while others might think my reaction was too apologetic.

But the reality is, these things matter. If we truly want to connect with people, we have to take these nuances into account, not only when sharing our faith but in any kind of discussion. Whether it's a debate, an argument, or simply a conversation where perspectives differ, body language and nonverbal communication play a crucial role in how we engage with others.

Man, full transparency: Walking away from that conversation, I remember having this overwhelming feeling of failure. And the truth is, I wasn't wrong about that. I had failed. But not because I didn't have the right arguments, wasn't prepared, or wasn't equipped. I failed because I wasn't cognizant of how my physical presence could become a barrier, how something as simple as touch or laughter could create a wall.

Up until then, I had underestimated the role that body language plays. I had spent so much of my life in ministry and in conversations zeroing in on what to say—curating responses, shaping ideas, finding angles—while overlooking one of the most important aspects of communication: the impact of posture and nonverbal cues.

The day before I wrote this chapter, I saw an example of how the power of body language plays out in real time in a viral clip from an episode of the TV show *The View* that featured Charlamagne tha God (please don't DM me about his name) and Whoopi Goldberg. After Charlamagne made a remark that rubbed Whoopi the wrong way, she responded by calling him "ridiculous." Instead of getting defensive, Charlamagne calmly clarified his intent, saying he hadn't meant to upset her. Whoopi's demeanor softened, and then she stood up, opened her arms, and gestured for him to come give her a hug.

I really loved this moment, because it could have gone in a completely different direction. It had all the elements of a heated argument, miscommunication, and hurt feelings, and the potential for a combustible exchange on national television. But instead of allowing tension to build, Charlamagne chose to clarify, and Whoopi, rather than escalating the situation, responded with a physical gesture that defused the moment.[1]

Now, someone might argue, "Yeah, but she didn't actually say, 'I'm sorry.'" And they wouldn't be wrong. But that's exactly the point of this chapter: to highlight the power of communication beyond words. Even though Whoopi didn't explicitly apologize, her body language spoke volumes, and the conversation was able to continue without hostility.

Albert Mehrabian's research on communication reveals that 55 percent of our communication is nonverbal, 38 percent is tone of voice, and only 7 percent comes from actual words.[2] This means that the way we carry ourselves, the way we stand, our facial expressions, and our gestures communicate far more than what we say. This is why body language can either build connections or create barriers, even when our words are well-intended.

We see this clearly in Jesus. The reason we know Jesus was approachable isn't just because of what He said but also because of how people responded to Him. The most marginalized—the lepers, the blind, the beggars, the prostitutes—felt comfortable calling out to Him, walking up to Him, even pressing through crowds just to touch Him. That alone tells us something about the statement His body made.

Take the blind man by the roadside, for instance. "Jesus, Son of David, have mercy on me!" Bartimaeus cried out from the outskirts of Jericho (Mark 10:46–52). The crowd tried to silence him, but Jesus stopped, turned, and called for him to come near. Jesus' entire posture—pausing, listening, and inviting—spoke volumes. He didn't wave the man off or keep walking; He welcomed the interruption.

Or consider the woman who anointed Jesus' feet. Luke tells us that a sinful woman (code for a "loose woman") entered a Pharisee's house where Jesus was dining, and "stood at His feet behind Him weeping;

and she began to wash His feet with her tears, and wiped them with the hair of her head; and she kissed His feet and anointed them with the fragrant oil" (Luke 7:36–38).

That was a bold, even scandalous, move. She wasn't just interrupting dinner; she was breaking cultural, religious, and moral boundaries. In those days, holy men didn't associate with women like her. A prostitute or loose woman wouldn't have come anywhere near a rabbi or a priest; she would've crossed the street to avoid such a man.[3] Listen, even today, people often feel that same discomfort around spiritual leaders. You can see it when folks censor themselves around pastors, priests, or church people ... lowering their voices, hiding their cigarette, apologizing for cursing, or pretending they don't drink. It's instinctive. Religious presence tends to make people self-conscious about certain behaviors and habits.

So what this woman did went against all the natural instincts of someone who knew she didn't measure up to the moral standards of the day. And yet, she went toward Jesus. She didn't run from Him. She approached, trembling but determined, because something about Him—His body language, His presence—told her she could.

He allowed her to come close, to touch Him, to pour out her sorrow and gratitude at His feet. His body language (still, receptive, and gracious) communicated what words never could: "You're safe with Me."

If you know anything about children, you know they're highly intuitive. They are not fully developed cognitively, so they rely heavily on intuition. They can sense warmth, or the lack of it, from a mile away. Children read energy better than adults do; they know when someone is genuinely kind or merely being tolerant. The fact that they felt drawn to Jesus says a lot—not only about His heart but also how He carried Himself. When the disciples tried to keep them away, Jesus rebuked them. "Let the little children come to Me, and do not forbid them; for of such is the kingdom of heaven" (Matt. 19:13–15).

He wasn't stiff, stoic, or unapproachable. He didn't stand with His chest puffed out in pride and piety. He didn't physically posture Himself as superior. No, He carried Himself in such a way that even the most overlooked, the most powerless, the most disregarded of society felt comfortable entering His space. That's how He was with the children: He invited them into His space.

If He had carried Himself as rigid, cold, and uninviting, they wouldn't have dared. If His posture had been one of pride or superiority, they would have assumed He was just like every other religious leader who saw them as nuisances. But they knew by watching Him, the way He moved and the way He engaged with people, that He was different. His body language told them that He was safe, that He was kind, that He was willing to be near them.

The lesson here is clear: Every part of us is communicating something. Our facial expressions, our tone, our posture, and maybe our choice of clothing all speak volumes about who we are and what we believe. When sharing our faith, we must be mindful not to create unintended barriers through nonverbal communication. Instead, we should strive to build bridges by expressing warmth, empathy, and genuine care through both our words and our body language.

Our actions can either hinder or enhance our message. By being aware of how we present ourselves, we ensure that our entire being—spoken words and silent signals—work together to invite others into a conversation of understanding, respect, and love. If we truly want to reflect Christ, we must preach the gospel not only with our lips but embody it with our lives.

CURIOUS CONVERSATION

"Christianity and Islam are basically the same."

I want to go back to that conversation I had in Leicester Square with the Muslim apologist. I want to look at the content of that exchange, the actual ideas that came up and the objections that were raised.

Having grown up in Philadelphia, where Islam is deeply woven into the cultural fabric, I've had countless dialogues with Muslims since my teenage years. In my high school alone, nearly half the student body was Muslim—young men and women who were fully garbed and deeply devoted. So when I met those apologists in London, it didn't feel foreign. It felt like home.

Islam is not some distant, exotic religion; it's one of the world's largest faiths, rich in tradition and discipline, and it has a growing presence in almost every part of the globe. That's why thoughtful, informed, and respectful conversations between Christians and Muslims now are more important than ever.

Let's revisit that exchange in London and explore what it looks like to have those conversations well.

Possible Dialogue

Them—Objection

Christianity and Islam are basically the same and lead to the same God. So what's the big difference?

You—Rude Response

Apparently you don't know much about either one if you think they're the same.

Why This Doesn't Work

Even if it's true, it doesn't help. Sarcasm, not to mention accusation, shuts the door on a conversation that could change a life.

Better Response

You—Affirm

I can understand why you'd say that. Both Christianity and Islam believe in one God, teach prayer, fasting, charity, and moral living. Both revere many of the same prophets and share elements of the Old Testament.

Empathize

I remember struggling with that same thought, wondering if all sincere people who worship God in whatever form they understand Him might eventually reach the same destination. It felt only fair. How could a just God condemn someone who honestly sought to honor Him?

Ask

Do you believe all religions lead to the same God, or that just Islam and Christianity do?

Answer

No, they do not lead to the same God. Because while both faiths are monotheistic, they part ways at the very center of their belief systems. The difference isn't peripheral—it's foundational.

In Christianity, Jesus died and rose again. In Islam, Jesus did not die and did not rise again. In Christianity, salvation is by grace through forgiveness. In Islam, salvation is by human effort and submission. In Christianity, humans are made in the image of God. In Islam, humans are servants of God. In Christianity, Jesus is God incarnate. In Islam, Jesus is a prophet—not divine.

These are not minor variations—they are theological contradictions. And contradictions cannot both be true. If both Christianity and Islam lead to God, then God Himself must be confused about His own nature and His own revelation. But the God of Scripture is not confused, indecisive, vague, or indifferent to truth.

Them—Rebuttal 1

I hear you, but Christianity still seems confusing. You say you believe in one God, but you talk about the Father, Son, and Holy Spirit, and last I checked, 1 + 1 + 1 = 3, not 1.

You—Affirm

Fair question. The logic doesn't seem to fit neatly.

Empathize

The Trinity has always been one of the most profound and complex mysteries in theology. Many of the analogies we use—like water being liquid, ice, and vapor; or an egg being shell, white, and yolk—may help a little, but ultimately all of them break down. None of them fully captures what it means for God to be one in essence yet three in person.

Ask

If I could show you that the concept of the Trinity doesn't emerge from Christian invention but from the very beginning of Scripture, would you be open to considering it?

Answer

Let's find common ground. Both Muslims and Christians affirm the book of Genesis as the account of creation—the beginning of all things. And in its very first chapter, we find something fascinating. God says, "Let Us make man in Our image" (Gen. 1:26). Us? Our? This is significant. The plural form raises an important question: Who is God talking to? Some have speculated angels or spiritual beings, but the text itself gives us clues.

The Spirit of God is present, "hovering over the face of the waters" (v. 2). The Father is implied as the initiator of creation. And John's Gospel confirms that the Son was also there—"Through him all things were made; without him nothing was made that has been made" (John 1:3 NIV). Yet Scripture still insists God is one.

Later, we see the same triune activity again—at Jesus' baptism (Matt. 3:16–17): The Father speaks from heaven, the Spirit descends like a dove, and the Son is baptized in the Jordan. Yet God remains one.

And Jesus Himself commands His followers to baptize "in the name" (singular) "of the Father and of the Son and of the Holy Spirit" (28:19). One name. Three persons.

Furthermore, each is identified in Scripture as God—the Father (Phil. 1:2), the Son (John 1:1; Heb. 1:8), and the Holy Spirit (Acts 5:3–4). So the triunity of God is threaded throughout the whole of Scripture.

Speaking respectfully, there is something I find interesting regarding the Trinity. Inasmuch as Islam critiques Christianity for affirming an eternal Word that enters the world, Islam itself affirms an eternal Word that enters the world. Islam teaches that the Qur'an is the eternal, uncreated Word of God—unmade, unoriginated, eternal. Yet the Qur'an Muslims hold in their hands is made of paper, ink, binding, glue. It can tear. It can burn. It can erode. It can be destroyed.

And herein lies the tension: Christianity teaches that the eternal Word of God entered the world in physical form as Jesus Christ. Islam teaches that the eternal Word of God enters the world in physical form as the Qur'an. Christianity teaches that Jesus' body, because it was physical, could bleed, suffer, and die. Islam teaches that the Qur'an, because it is physical, can tear, decay, and be destroyed. In both cases, the eternal Word enters the material world.

So Islam must grapple with something it critiques: the eternal Word entering creation. It quietly affirms what it openly denies. And acknowledging that tension opens the door to a deeper, more honest dialogue about who God truly is and how He reveals Himself.

But I understand why it still feels confusing. As people say, "The math isn't mathing." 1 + 1 + 1 = 3—which is why many assume that Christianity teaches three gods. You would be right, if addition were the only formula available. But it's not. There is also multiplication, where 1 x 1 x 1 = 1.

That's the better picture: one divine nature expressed through three coequal, coeternal persons. The Trinity is not a contradiction—it is a revelation. And when you compare the Christian claim with the internal categories Islam already affirms about Allah, the Qur'an, and Muhammad, the Christian framework is not only coherent, it is more theologically consistent.

Them—Rebuttal 2

Okay, but you keep quoting the Bible, and yet the Bible has been corrupted.

You—Affirm

I've heard that claim many times.

Empathize

I get it—it's hard to believe any text handled by humans could remain pure.

Ask

What makes you confident the Qur'an is perfect but the Bible isn't?

Answer

Here's the irony: The Qur'an itself affirms the authority of the Bible.

- Surah 5:46–47 calls the gospel "guidance and light."
- Surah 10:94 instructs Muhammad, "If you are in doubt ... ask those who have read the Scripture before you."
- Surah 3:3 says Allah "revealed the Torah and the Gospel."

Islam came roughly six centuries after Christianity,[4] yet it draws from the prophets, narratives, and theological framework already present in Scripture (Surah 3 [Āl 'Imrān]; Surah 19 [Maryam]; Surah 5:46; Surah 2:136). If the Bible were truly corrupted, then Islam's foundation collapses—because its entire understanding of God, revelation, and prophecy depends on those earlier texts being trustworthy.

So the real issue isn't textual corruption; it's theological tension. The Bible points forward to Jesus as the eternal Son of God. The Qur'an points backward to Jesus as a mere prophet. Both cannot be right. And if both cannot be right, then both cannot lead to the same God.

KEYS FOR THE CONVERSATION

If you can remember these keys, you'll carry the heart of this chapter and the tools you'll need into every conversation.

1. What You Need to Know

Your body communicates just as strongly as your words. The way you stand, the tone you use, your facial expression, your eye contact, and your overall presence shape how your message is received. People instinctively read nonverbal cues, and they decide whether to open up or shut down based on what your body is saying long before they process your actual words.

2. What You Need to Do

Be intentional about the nonverbal signals you send. Pay close attention to your tone, posture, facial expression, distance, and eye contact.

Practice having meaningful or difficult conversations and observe your natural tendencies—what you project, how your body reacts, and what you may be communicating without realizing it. The more aware you are, the more effectively your body will support your message instead of contradicting it.

3. Who You Need to Become

Become someone who carries a calm, grounded, welcoming presence—a person whose posture is open, relaxed, and warm rather than tense or defensive. When your body puts people at ease, you remove barriers and create a space where real conversation can happen.

Chapter 5

THE GOSPEL I NEVER KNEW

We are always in danger of seeing only one corner of God's truth and mistaking it for the whole.

In the spirit of C. S. Lewis

Breaking Free from a Reductionist View of the Gospel

I hadn't shared my faith in nearly two years.

Not on purpose. Not out of rebellion. I wasn't angry at God. I wasn't even drifting. At least, not consciously. It just ... happened.

A few years back, this question quietly surfaced in my mind: *Wait ... when was the last time I actually talked to someone about Jesus—someone who doesn't already believe?*

I sat with it.

And the more I thought about it, the more I realized I couldn't remember the last time I had shared the hope that shaped my life. And that realization wasn't just startling; it was sobering. Sharing my faith is part of my calling. It's literally what I do. I'm an evangelist.

A communicator. A bridge builder. This is in my DNA. So what was happening?

At first, I chalked it up to life—scheduling, busyness, rhythms, projects. But something about that felt too convenient. Too surface level. The longer I sat with the silence, the more I began to wonder: Maybe it wasn't something that had already changed ... maybe it was something that needed to.

The Way It Used to Be

I grew up in a time when evangelism was war.

Not in the hostile, hateful sense, but in the sense that it was a clash of ideas. A battle of beliefs. A war of worldviews.

Especially in Philly, you couldn't share your faith without expecting some pushback. We were surrounded by competing ideologies—Islam, Hebrew Israelite teachings, the Five-Percent Nation. It was everywhere. That was the climate. That was the conversation. That was the culture.

And hip-hop was the megaphone.

People forget this now, but hip-hop was once far more philosophical than flashy. It wasn't about Bentleys and bottles; it was about belief systems. It preached. It questioned. It taught. It pushed Afrocentric thought, exposed listeners to ancient philosophies, and challenged religious traditions head-on. And it had the streets' ear.

So evangelism back then wasn't about convincing someone to consider a new idea; it was about confronting someone who already had one. We weren't talking to blank slates. We were talking to people with frameworks. Concrete ideas. Sacred texts of their own.

And our conversations reflected that: Scripture for scripture, ideology for ideology, logic for logic.

It was intense. But it was clear.

Then ... something shifted.

It's not that people stopped believing; it's that belief stopped being about truth. And in a culture where everyone's truth is valid, the gospel doesn't sound offensive anymore—it sounds irrelevant.

The fight moved. The questions changed. The ideologies blurred. The sharp edges of theological conviction gave way to the fog of moral autonomy. People weren't saying, "I believe something different." They were saying, "Who are you to tell me anything at all?"

Hedonism and hyperindividualism slowly replaced the combative climate I once knew. Instead of facing off against well-formed arguments, we began navigating shrugging shoulders, distracted minds, and emotionally charged deconstruction.

It's not that people stopped believing; it's that belief stopped being about truth. And in a culture where everyone's truth is valid, the gospel doesn't sound offensive anymore—it sounds irrelevant.

This was unfamiliar territory.

I knew how to stand toe-to-toe with people who had convictions. People who had something they were willing to argue for. People who knew their beliefs—even if they were wrong—and were ready to defend them.

I thrived in those environments.

At the first college I attended, before I realized that theology was the path I was supposed to be on, I was a music major. But let's just say I wasn't exactly faithful to the curriculum.

I take no pride in this, since it was definitely irresponsible, but I spent most of my days skipping classes and debating Muslims on campus. All day. Every day. In the cafeteria. In dorm rooms. In front of buildings. If someone had a different worldview, I was there. Engaged. Passionate. Locked in.

And it goes without saying: I failed school that first year.

That was the downside.

But the upside? That's how I figured out what I was really called to do. That's how I ended up in Bible college. Those debates awakened something deep in me. They revealed my passion for truth, for Scripture, for helping people wrestle with hard questions. I realized I was wired for that.

This kind of engagement was my comfort zone. That was evangelism as I understood it: intense, intellectual, and even confrontational, if necessary. And I knew how to handle those kinds of conversations. I could talk to people from other religions. I could reason with them, show them the flaws in their logic, walk them through Scripture, make the case for Jesus.

But what was happening now? This was something else. This was new. This was foggy. We were shifting.

These weren't pre-Christian conversations anymore, where people had never heard the gospel and needed clarity. And it wasn't Christian-Christian, where people already believed and just needed sharpening or encouragement. This was post-Christian.[1]

People weren't just uninformed; they were disillusioned. Suspicious. Jaded. Their resistance wasn't about evidence; it was about experience. They'd seen too much, heard too much, felt too hurt, been too disappointed. It wasn't that they had competing truth claims. It was that they weren't sure anymore that truth was even a thing.

And I didn't know how to engage that.

For the first time in my life, the playbook I'd relied on didn't seem to apply. I couldn't just out-argue this. I couldn't quote enough scriptures to fix it. I couldn't logic my way through someone's wounds.

What used to be a conversation about facts had become a conversation about trust.

So ... now what?

I had spent most of my life learning how to contend for the faith, often against people from other religions or belief systems. But this was different. I wasn't just engaging Muslims, Jehovah's Witnesses, or atheists. I was talking to people who didn't claim anything at all. Not "religious others," but people who had grown up with the idea of Christianity in the background. The soundtrack of their childhood might've included gospel radio, Kirk Franklin, church once or twice a year, or Trinity Broadcasting Network playing in the living room while their grandma braided their hair. These weren't foreign or hostile to the faith ... they were familiar. Too familiar.

Some of them had been raised in Christian environments. And as I explained the gospel, they could almost say it with me. Not because they fully understood it but because they had heard it before. So now what? How do you evangelize someone who feels like they've already "graduated" from Christianity? How do you preach the gospel to someone who's tired of the pitch?

What happened next was nothing but God.

The answer came, not immediately but through a process. Through wrestling. Through frustration. Through prayer. And then, through a class that would change everything.

I haven't mentioned it yet, but I attended the Oxford Centre for Christian Apologetics in England. One semester, I took a class I didn't think I needed. It was about ways to present the gospel, and I thought I'd heard every gospel presentation there was: the Romans Road, the Four Spiritual Laws, the *Purpose Driven Life* approach, the Reformed "God is holy and just" structure, every possible framing of the gospel. The class was taught by Professor John Dickson, and I was not expecting anything new.

I was wrong.

This wasn't information. This was revelation.

It was a paradigm shift that changed my entire approach to sharing the faith.

John began by talking about how the word *gospel* (*euangélion* in Greek) wasn't originally a religious word.[2] It was a secular term. It wasn't first used to mean "good news." It originally meant "*breaking* news." It was the word used in ancient times to make a royal announcement. When a king won a war or a new emperor was crowned, they'd send heralds throughout the empire to announce the news: "A new king reigns!" That announcement was called a gospel. It wasn't about spiritual transformation; it was about making a history-shaping, kingdom-shaking proclamation.

That wrecked me.

Because it reframed the way I saw the gospel, not just as good news but as breaking news: *The King has come*. That changed everything.

But that was just the beginning.

John Dickson then walked us through how the early church understood the gospel—not just as Jesus' death, burial, and resurrection (as important as that is), but as the entirety of Jesus' life. That's why the Gospels—Matthew, Mark, Luke, and John—are called the gospel. Singular. Not "the Gospels about Jesus" but the gospel of Jesus. Because the gospel is His whole life—His teachings, His miracles, His parables, His compassion, His suffering, His authority, His confrontation with religious hypocrisy, His embodiment of the kingdom, His fulfillment of Israel's story ... and then His death and resurrection.[3]

Paul's summary in 1 Corinthians 15—"Christ died for our sins according to the Scriptures" (v. 3)—was exactly that: a summary of the gospel that had already been received and proclaimed. It wasn't the whole story. It was the climax.

That blew the lid off everything for me.

Because for years, I had been starting at the end.

I was robbing people of the entire story of Jesus. Every time I'd shared the gospel, I started with the cross. But the cross is one of the final chapters of the Gospels, not the first. And I realized: Maybe that's why it wasn't landing anymore. Maybe that's why people felt like they had heard it before. Because I was treating the gospel like a sales pitch—and they were tired of being pitched to.

This changed the way I engaged.

It gave me room to breathe.

I no longer felt pressure to hurry up and "get to the four points." I didn't have to rush to the punchline. Because I now saw the whole life of Jesus as gospel. And that gave me so much more to work with. I could have a conversation about money and bring in Jesus. I could talk about justice—and bring in Jesus. I could talk about rest or relationships or purpose—and bring in Jesus. Because He's not just the one who died. He's the one who lived: perfectly, powerfully, compassionately, and beautifully. And that life is part of the gospel.

I'll give you an example.

One day in Oxford, I had a flat tire and went into a bike shop to get it fixed. The guy behind the counter asked me what I was doing in town, and when I told him I was studying theology, the conversation took a turn. He lit up with objections: Christianity is antiscience, the Bible isn't credible, religion is a crutch ... all the classics. And I was ready. I was in school for apologetics, after all! So I had my answers. But nothing I said seemed to move him. It was like he'd heard it all before.

Honestly, I was tired. I wanted to go home. But as I turned to leave, he said something unexpected: "Wanna come out back? Let's keep talking. I'm gonna smoke."

I hesitated ... I grew up in the hood, and I'd seen too many mafia movies. But this was Oxford, England, where C. S. Lewis had spent his adult life. So I followed him to the back alley of the bike shop, and we kept talking. Somewhere in the conversation, I remembered John Dickson's class. I remembered the life of Jesus. And I asked the guy: "If God exists, what do you think He mostly wants from people? Like, what's His highest priority?"

He thought for a moment and said, "To be decent. To be moral."

I said, "Can I tell you how Jesus responded when someone gave Him that exact same answer?"

He nodded.

I told him the story of the rich young ruler. The man who listed all his moral achievements but walked away sad. Because being "good" wasn't the point (Matt. 19:16–26; Mark 10:17–22; Luke 18:18–23). And then I unpacked the story a little. For the first time in our conversation … he got quiet. For ten minutes, he didn't say a word. He just listened.

It wasn't my argument that reached him. It was Jesus.

There will always be something about Jesus that commands attention. Even among skeptics. There's still something about His words that hushes the room. Something about His presence that can't be ignored.

I think about that moment in the synagogue when He read Isaiah 61 and said, "Today this Scripture is fulfilled in your hearing" (Luke 4:21). The people stared at Him. They were frozen. And that same authority still rests on Him today. Which is why appealing to His life matters so much.

It opens doors that our arguments can't.

And the best part? This doesn't apply just to religious conversations. Jesus has spoken to every area of life—money, sex, power, politics, rest, forgiveness, leadership, trauma, relationships, family, identity. So now, instead of feeling pressure to pivot every conversation into a theological sales pitch, I can just bring Jesus into it. Naturally. Authentically. Confidently.

Because the gospel is not just how He died.

It's how He lived.

For years, I'd been starting at the end of the story, leading people to the cross. I didn't realize how much I was reducing the gospel to a set of talking points: Sin. Death. Substitution. Resurrection.

All true, though, right? Necessary. Powerful. But incomplete, if we leave out His life.

The revelation that the gospel includes the life of Jesus wasn't just a new angle. It was a new framework. It reminded me that the gospel isn't only an altar call. It's not merely a private invitation to escape judgment. It's a royal announcement. A kingdom proclamation. The King has come—and that changes everything.

No, I'm not walking away from the cross. I'm not diluting the message; I'm expanding it. I still believe that the gospel, as Paul says, is "the power of God unto salvation" (Rom. 1:16 KJV). That hasn't changed. That won't change. What has changed is that I've stopped rushing. Stopped skipping past the life of Jesus just to get to the death of Jesus. Stopped forcing spiritual conversations to crescendo before they even breathe.

Because when you embrace the full scope of who Jesus is and not just what He did, you realize something powerful: His life is also an open door.

It's not just a moral example. It's a bridge. A starting point. A way to enter real conversations about justice, pain, leadership, humility, culture, identity, power, peace, presence, sacrifice. It gives us room to linger with people. To walk with them. To meet them in the everyday and allow Jesus, the way He lived, to speak first. Because sometimes ... that's where the gospel begins.

The life of Christ, breaking in, breaking open, breaking ground.

And when that happens, the cross doesn't lose its power. It becomes even more beautiful—because by the time you get to that part of the story, you've seen the One who hung there.

CURIOUS CONVERSATION

"Christianity is a religion with a book full of fairy tales. I believe in science."

Earlier in the chapter, I mentioned the conversation I had with the guy working in the bike shop. One of his biggest objections to Christianity was that it was antiscience. And honestly, that's a common one. Especially in the West, where empirical thinking still rules the day. If it can't be tasted, touched, measured, or repeated in a lab, it doesn't count. That's the default.

So to people shaped by that perspective, the Bible starts to feel like a fairy-tale book. Miracles feel like magic tricks. And Christians? We're seen as people who blindly believe things that make no rational sense.

They'll say things like:

"You still believe in that stuff?"

"You don't really believe in miracles, do you?"

"Religion is for people who can't deal with reality."

To them, believing in the supernatural is the same as being anti-reason. Antiprogress. Antiscience.

So I figured it was worth zooming in on. Because this objection isn't just academic—it's emotional. For some people, science is more than a method. It's a worldview. It's what replaced faith. So how do you start that conversation?

Let's walk through it.

Possible Dialogue

Them—Objection

Christianity is a fairy tale. I believe in science—things we can actually prove, not ancient miracle stories.

You—Rude Response

Well, apparently science isn't helping you think straight.

Why This Doesn't Work

It mocks the person instead of addressing their concern. Once someone feels dismissed, they stop listening—and the conversation ends.

Better Response

You—Affirm

That's a common concern. Thoughtful people have wrestled with this for centuries.

Empathize

Science feels dependable because it deals with what we can measure and repeat. Christianity involves the supernatural, miracles, and ancient texts. So I understand why the two might appear incompatible.

Ask

What led you to believe Christianity and science contradict each other? Was it something specific you encountered or more of an assumption?

Answer

One of the most common misconceptions is that faith floats above the real world while science deals with what is solid and trustworthy. But Scripture consistently ties faith to what can be seen, examined, and reasoned about. This is why Paul writes, "Since the creation of the world God's invisible qualities ... have been clearly seen, being understood from what has been made" (Rom. 1:20 NIV). Paul is showing that God's invisible nature becomes visible through creation. That is observational reasoning, which is foundational to scientific inquiry.

It's interesting because people often accuse Christians of blind faith, but many naturalistic explanations require more unsupported belief than Christianity does. When Christians look at the world, we reason from effect to Cause, design to Designer, intelligence to Intelligent Source. Those categories match everyday human experience.

By contrast, a purely naturalistic explanation requires belief in everything arising from nothing, life emerging from nonlife, consciousness arising from matter, and order emerging from undirected processes. There is no precedent in ordinary human experience for any of that. We see an iPhone, and no one concludes it assembled itself. We see a painting, and no one assumes it appeared without a painter. Nothing in our lived experience points toward complex order emerging without an ordering mind. That isn't religion; it's basic reasoning. And the Christian explanation fits that reasoning more naturally than its alternatives.

To take it a step further, modern science did not grow out of atheism; it grew out of Christian theism. The founders of modern science—Newton, Kepler, Boyle, Faraday, Maxwell, Mendel—believed the universe was intelligible because it was created by an intelligent God. They expected order because they believed in a Lawgiver. Christianity wasn't competing with science; it provided the framework that made scientific discovery possible. So the idea that Christianity is antiscience isn't historical. That's a modern assumption, not a factual one.

Possible Response

Them—Rebuttal 1

Christianity still feels like mythology. Miracles sound like fairy tales.

You—Rude Response

I'd rather believe in a fairy tale than believe in nothing.

Why This Doesn't Work

It ignores the real intellectual tension the person is experiencing.

Better Response

You—Affirm

I understand why miracles are hard to accept. Most of us don't witness them daily.

Empathize

And I get it—I'm naturally a skeptical person myself. So I understand why supernatural claims feel like a stretch.

Ask

Are you rejecting the credibility of the miracle accounts themselves, or do you hold the assumption that anything supernatural must be impossible?

Answer

People often compare Christianity to fairy tales because miracles sound unbelievable. But fairy tales don't involve real people, real historical settings, or geographically verifiable locations (Matt. 2:1). Christianity is rooted in actual places you can visit, real historical figures you can research, and real events documented by eyewitnesses (1 Cor. 15:3–8), some of whom were sympathetic while others were skeptical or even openly hostile.

But that isn't enough to settle the issue. After all, Spider-Man "lives" in New York, a real city you can visit, but he's no more real than Santa Claus. So the real issue isn't geography. It's worldview.

If someone begins with the assumption that *only* what can be tasted, touched, heard, seen, or measured is real, then every miracle will automatically sound fictional. Not because of evidence, but because their starting point forbids any supernatural explanation. So the first question isn't *"Are miracles believable?"* The first question is *"Does your worldview even allow them to be possible?"*

Because if miracles are impossible by definition, no amount of evidence will ever matter.

But if a person is willing to say, *"Okay, it's at least possible that something exists beyond the material world,"* then they must consider the credibility of eyewitness accounts, the historical reliability of

Scripture, and testimonies from people who were not predisposed to believe.

There's another layer too: A worldview that denies anything beyond matter struggles to account for consciousness, morality, meaning, the immaterial laws of logic, the fine-tuning of the universe, or even the existence of rational thought. These are not fairy tales. These are philosophical realities that any worldview must wrestle with.

So the debate is not simply about whether Christianity is unbelievable. The deeper issue is whether your worldview makes room for anything beyond the material world. If God exists, miracles are not violations of natural law—they are the actions of the One who wrote the laws. That means the real tension isn't "science versus Christianity." It's *materialism versus theism*—two fundamentally different ways of understanding reality.

KEYS FOR THE CONVERSATION

Every chapter has a lot of moving pieces, but if you can remember these keys, you'll carry the heart of this chapter and the tools you'll need into every conversation.

1. What You Need to Know

You are not compromising, changing, or diluting the gospel by understanding it in a fuller, richer way. You're actually being faithful to Scripture. Many people were introduced to an oversimplified gospel—true but thin. But because a partial understanding of the gospel forms an incomplete picture of who Christ is, what you're doing here is recovering the depth, the breadth, the beauty, and the fullness of the gospel as Scripture presents it.

2. What You Need to Do

Introduce and/or reintroduce people to the gospel in its fullness. Listen for the gaps: What were they taught? What were they never shown? What were they never invited into? Your goal is to clarify and highlight a more comprehensive vision of Jesus—one that speaks to the whole of life.

3. Who You Need to Become

Become a person whose life widens the story of Jesus instead of shrinking it. Be someone whose presence helps people see a fuller, more integrated picture of Christ.

Chapter 6

SAY IT WITH YOUR CHEST (WHEN IT'S TIME TO BE BOLD)

A time comes when silence is betrayal.

Martin Luther King Jr., "Beyond Vietnam" speech

Culture Is Drawn to Bold Voices

In this cultural moment, the voices people listen to the most are not always the most polished or even the most principled. They're the clearest.

Look around. The more assertive, unfiltered, controversial, and confrontational someone is, the more likely they are to cut through the noise and get people's attention. That's the world we live in now. Platforms aren't given just to the articulate; they're also given to the audacious.

It's why people like Andrew Tate, Candace Owens, the late Kevin Samuels, and Kanye West have been able to build massive audiences. Not because everything they say is true but because they speak with conviction.

They speak boldly. And in a time when many messages are filtered through PR teams, vague slogans, or sanitized sound bites, people are hungry for something that sounds like truth, even if it's only a shadow of it.

Now let me be clear: I'm not holding any of these personalities up as role models. I don't agree with everything they say, and I'm not suggesting we take our cues from their content.

But if we're honest, there's something to learn from their conviction.

They know how to *say it with their chest* (with courage and conviction). And sometimes, the church could use a bit more of that. Not the arrogance, not the abrasiveness, but the assurance.

I recently heard Kanye West say in an interview that 60 to 70 percent of the people who once called him crazy now say, "He's just telling you exactly what's going on."[1] That might seem like bravado, but it speaks to something real: People are starving for clarity. For something to call truth. For someone to stand up and say what others only hint at.

And speaking of Ye, there was brief moment he and I had together some years back that bolsters my point.

During a festival in Canada, both Kanye West and I were performing; same festival but different stages. The next morning, we happened to end up on the same flight back into the States. I was near the gate with two of my brothers, facing away from them. I heard them talking to someone but didn't realize who it was until one of my boys tapped me on the shoulder and said, "Look."

I turned around, and there they were, having a full-blown conversation with Kanye West.

I'll be honest: Initially, I was stunned. I had to compose myself. And immediately the internal conversation started: *How should I introduce myself? Do I just say I'm a rapper? Do I clarify that I'm a* Christian *rapper*? At the time, there was so much debate about how tightly we should hold on to that label. I was committed to wearing it boldly, but now, standing in front of Kanye, I felt the tension.

Would saying "Christian hip-hop artist" make me seem small? Would it make him dismiss me?

All this flashed through my mind in a matter of moments.

But then I made a decision: I was going to say it with my chest.

"Hey," I said. We talked a bit, and I shook his hand. "I go by Da' T.R.U.T.H., and I'm a Christian hip-hop artist."

Needless to say, I braced myself for whatever reaction might come—mockery, indifference ... who knew?

But to my surprise, Kanye dropped his head, slumped his shoulders, stared at the floor, and said, "It's been such a long time since I've had a relationship with God."

In that moment, I was taken aback. That was not the response I was expecting. Yet I was equally overwhelmed with gratitude that I had stuck to my gut.

Had I played it safe, had I just said, "I rap," there would have been no moment of sobriety. No crack in the door. No opening for reflection.

That moment showed me the value not only of "saying it afraid," so to speak, but to be wary of that fear, because fear can disguise itself as wisdom and strategy. And had I listened to that fear-dressed-as-false wisdom, I would've missed out on the opportunity to say something to someone who desperately needed a nudge from God.

After that unexpected encounter with Kanye, I couldn't shake the thought that moments to speak truth rarely come gift wrapped. Instead, they slip into everyday spaces—airport gates, lunch tables, DMs—and whisper, *Will you stay safe, or will you stand firm?*

Think about it.

How many times in a single week do we pass by opportunities to say what matters most? We freeze, we soften, we delay. And clarity dies the slow death of caution.

This is a constant fight. But I get it: It's not always so simple. It's not always black and white. It takes discernment, wisdom, and an understanding of what's necessary for the moment.

A Time for Everything

Now I know what you might be thinking.

You've been tracking with everything I've talked about in this book so far: the nuance, the diplomacy, the empathy. You're finally starting to settle into that rhythm: listening first, answering with grace, leading with love.

And now you hear me urging you, "Say it with your chest."

So naturally, you're asking, "Okay ... that's a shift and I get it, but how do I know when to do what?"

When is it time to speak with fire instead of finesse?

When is it time to flip the tables, to press harder, to get fierce?

When is it time to, like Paul, oppose someone to their face (Gal. 2:11 NIV)?

Ecclesiastes says, "To everything there is a season, a time for every purpose under heaven" (3:1). There's a time to build and a time to break down, a time to whisper and a time to roar. And no one captured this balance better than Jesus Christ Himself.

How?

Jesus dealt gently with individuals but firmly with institutions.

He handled people with grace but agendas with fire.

When Jesus met someone sincerely searching, open, or wounded, He led with gentleness and grace. But when He faced systems or leaders promoting deception and hypocrisy, His tone changed. He confronted directly, even sharply.

You can see this contrast throughout the gospels.

With the woman at the well in John 4:4–29, He didn't condemn her. He asked for water (v. 7) and offered her "living water" (vv. 13–14), and when He finally addressed her brokenness, He did so with dignity: "You have well said, 'I have no husband,' for you have had five husbands, and the one whom you now have is not your husband" (vv. 17–18).

No public shaming, no anger—just truth wrapped in invitation.

And by the end of the conversation, she's running back to town, saying, "Come, see a Man who told me all things that I ever did" (v. 29).

But when Jesus dealt with agendas, like the harmful practices of the Pharisees and the religious elite who misled others, His tone was very different.

In Matthew 23, He said things like:

- "Woe to you, teachers of the law and Pharisees, you hypocrites! You shut the door of the kingdom of heaven in people's faces" (v. 13 NIV).

- "You are like whitewashed tombs which indeed appear beautiful outwardly, but inside are full of dead men's bones" (v. 27).
- "You snakes! You brood of vipers! How will you escape being condemned to hell?" (v. 33 NIV).

Same Jesus.

Different tone.

Different purpose.

He was tender with individuals but fierce with institutions.

He comforted sinners but confronted systems.

He spoke gently to the broken—but with fire to the Pharisees, because their teaching was toxic. They weren't just wrong; they were dangerous.

That's the example He left for us. When dealing with individuals, lead with gentleness. Be diplomatic. Be discerning. Be patient. That's when listening matters most and compassion and relationship do the heavy lifting.

But when you're dealing with agendas, that's different. You don't negotiate with deception; you confront it. You don't reason with systems that are poisoning people; you resist them.

That's why Elijah, in the face of 450 prophets of Baal, shouted, "How long will you waver between two opinions?" (1 Kings 18:21 NIV).

Paul wore that same mantle when he opposed Peter "to his face" (Gal. 2:11 NIV).

Martin Luther had to protest corruption in the church. He wasn't fighting a man; he was fighting a machine. Martin Luther King Jr. wasn't just pleading for kindness; he was demanding transformation.

He wasn't arguing with individuals; he was opposing systems that legalized injustice. And in our generation, that tension lives on in hip-hop culture where Dee-1 is on the front line pushing back against an industry narrative that glorifies death, misogyny, greed, and moral decay.

And that's the difference.

When you're dealing with individuals, you converse. When you're confronting destructive, toxic agendas, you confront.

So when Christian nationalism starts sounding more like supremacy than servanthood; when liberation theology exalts race over redemption; when LGBTQ+ activism insists on reshaping the moral compass of children; when hip-hop glorifies murder, misogyny, and nihilism; and when deception dresses up as enlightenment—that's when it's time to dial it up.

Not out of anger. Out of love. Out of a zeal to protect what's sacred. Out of conviction that silence in the face of deception is a form of complicity.

There is a time to be gentle, but there's also a time to drive the money changers out of the temple. A time to raise your voice. A time to stand your ground. A time to fight for the truth. And wisdom is knowing the difference.

But here's the thing: Courage and confrontation are costly.

Courage and confrontation are expensive virtues. They cost applause, opportunity, sometimes safety. But the price of silence is higher—it costs integrity.

Paul's confession still stings the modern ego: "If I were still trying to please people, I would not be a servant of Christ" (Gal. 1:10 NIV). We love to tweet, "I don't care what people think." But often, that's exactly what we want them to think. The craving for approval is human; the worship of it is bondage.

If no one else understood this, Stephen the martyr did. He understood firsthand that man's praise and God's approval are sometimes incompatible. His sermon in Acts 7 was both a history lesson and indictment. The crowd responded with stones to kill him, but heaven responded with honor: "Look! I see the heavens opened and the Son of Man standing at the right hand of God!" (v. 56).

The theological implications of this moment stop me every time. Everywhere else in Scripture, Jesus is described as sitting at the right hand of the Father. He's sitting because the work of redemption is finished. Figuratively speaking, the priests of the Old Covenant could never sit down because their work was never done. But Jesus, the Great High Priest, *sat*—signaling that the sacrifice was complete and the mission accomplished.

The craving for approval is human; the worship of it is bondage.

Yet in Stephen's moment of courage, heaven broke protocol.

The King stood.

Heaven rose to its feet to honor a man the world was tearing apart. Jesus, who sits to rule, stood to receive. Stephen didn't die trending; he died applauded by heaven.

That is the paradox of courage for Jesus: The world may cancel you, but heaven claps for you. The crowd may shrink back, but Christ stands up.

The standing ovation of Christ was heaven's way of honoring Stephen's courage. But there's another layer to that reward.

The Bible says that as the mob picked up stones, "the witnesses laid down their clothes at the feet of a young man named Saul" (Acts 7:58). Paul the apostle (then known as Saul) was there. Not only present but leading the charge (8:3; 26:9–11).

Of course, Saul's conversion on the Damascus Road was all God: sovereign, dramatic, unmistakably divine (9:1–19). I can't help but imagine that in those three days of blindness, as Saul sat in silence, the memory of Stephen—radiant, fearless, praying for his killers—must have stayed with him (7:59–60; 9:9).

And I would imagine that memory inspired his own courage later in life, as God was shaping him into the chief apostle of the early church (9:15; Gal. 1:23–24). So although it was costly, the reward was greater than the cost. As Jesus stood for Stephen, Saul was on the trajectory of being transformed (7:55–56; 9:20–22).

That moment also reminds us that courage doesn't just echo in eternity—it reverberates through history.

When heaven stood, earth was changed. Our faithfulness never ends with us; it sets something in motion (Heb. 12:1; Matt. 5:16). If Stephen's courage inspired Saul—who became the apostle Paul—then we can trace the ripple effects across the centuries … all the way to you and me. The gospel that reached continents and shaped civilizations began with moments like that—with ordinary believers willing to stand when it cost them everything (Acts 1:8; 2 Tim. 2:3). From the early church fathers—men like Athanasius, Irenaeus, and Origen, who confronted Gnosticism head-on;[2] and Tertullian, who defended the doctrine of the Trinity (Jude 1:3)—to Philip Mitchell, Jackie Hill Perry—a poet and teacher who shared her story in *Gay Girl, Good God*[3]—and Dee-1.

In a generation that is addicted to affirmation and allergic to conflict, these voices, along with many others—using their pulpit, podcast, music, and entertainment platforms—have decided to be salt and light in the midst of a crooked and perverse generation (Phil. 2:15; Matt. 5:13–16). With a resolve to not just be gentle as doves but bold as lions (Matt. 10:16; Prov. 28:1), we are pushing back against the evils and ideologies that distort truth and destroy lives. And like those before us, our courage will echo—not just in heaven but across generations (Rev. 12:11).

CURIOUS CONVERSATION

"Do you believe being gay is a sin?"

Before we get to the objection itself, let's set the stage.

Sex and gender are topics that require extraordinary care. A good example is Jackie Hill Perry's book, *Gay Girl, Good God*, which is filled with honesty, tension, and grace. Conversations about sexuality in our generation are uniquely charged because almost everything in today's culture orbits around sex, identity, entertainment, politics, marketing, and self-worth. It's everywhere. And it's one of the very few subjects that can get you "canceled" from both sides.

Lean too far right ... you're bigoted, hateful, homophobic.

Lean too far left ... you're compromised, unbiblical, progressive.

It's a cultural catch-22.

But beneath all that—the hashtags, anger, defensiveness, fear, and cultural pressure—people are still asking: *What does God actually think about all this? And how do I respond with both compassion and conviction?*

This isn't about winning debates; it's about learning to speak truth with empathy in one of the most difficult conversations of our cultural moment. Let's walk through it.

Possible Dialogue

Them—Objection

Do you believe being gay is a sin?

You—Rude Response

Not only is it a sin—it's the worst of them.

Why This Doesn't Work

This reduces a deeply personal, emotional question into a hierarchy-of-sin argument that Scripture never makes. It reinforces the stereotype that Christians are obsessed with homosexuality, and it ignores the reality that *every human being is sexually broken* in some way. It answers a tender, heart-level question with a hammer.

Better Response

You—Affirm

I know the LGBTQ+ community and the church have not exactly seen eye to eye. So I completely understand the place this question is coming from.

Empathize

And I also know this topic has often been treated like the worst of all sins—and that's just not true.

Ask

I'd imagine this is a question you've wrestled with and talked to others about, maybe even to Christians. So let me ask you: *Based on your understanding of who you think God is and your own story, where have you landed?*

Answer

Before we talk about sexuality, we need to talk about sin.

Sin isn't just rule breaking.

It's anything—thought, word, or deed—that falls short of God's standard, rebels against His design, or elevates our will over His. Augustine described sin as "a disorder of loves."[4] I think that nails it. All of us have our loves out of order—our desires, our ambitions, our intentions. When love for self outruns love for God, things fracture.

We see that disorder everywhere: in politics, religion, social media, entertainment. Everything is out of order.

And that includes our sexuality.

Every one of us is sexually broken in some way. Heterosexual or homosexual, none of us has desires that perfectly reflect God's design (Mark 7:21–23).

So is same-sex behavior a sin?

Scripture teaches that sexual expression outside male-female marriage falls outside God's design (Gen. 1:27; 2:24; Rom. 1:26–27).

But that truth does not exist in isolation. It sits alongside an even greater truth: *Every human being is loved, pursued, and invited to grace by God.*

Them—Rebuttal 1

Okay, but why do Christians care so much about who I sleep with? What I do in my private life shouldn't matter to anybody.

You—Affirm

I get it. You want to be left alone to live your life in peace. You're basically saying, "Live and let live."

Empathize

I'm a private person myself, so I really do understand where you're coming from.

Ask

Let me ask you something: Do you think Christians wake up every day looking for ways to talk about this, like we're trying to police people's lives? Or do you think maybe we're responding to what's already happening around us?

Answer

Here's what I believe: Most Christians aren't trying to police anyone's bedroom.

We're responding to a cultural conversation that has become impossible to ignore.

In past generations, topics like sex and identity stayed private. Today, sexuality is everywhere—movies, schools, cartoons, workplace policies, political debates. Kids come home confused. Teens ask questions. Culture is constantly discipling everyone.

Christians talk about this largely out of necessity, not obsession.

We respond because we're being asked directly and indirectly all the time.

But the heart of Christianity isn't moral nitpicking. It's introducing people, regardless of sexuality, to the love and transforming power of Christ.

Them—Rebuttal 2

Okay, but if homosexuality is a sin and I'm gay, does that mean you believe I'm going to hell?

You—Affirm

I have to be honest—that's a really tough question. And I do understand why you'd ask it.

Empathize

I would imagine that having that question looming over you is pretty heavy.

Ask

Can I ask you something? When you think about God and about yourself, what do you think He thinks of you?

Answer

There are a few layers to this answer, so here's where I'll start:

The Bible does say that "the unrighteous will not inherit the kingdom of God," and it includes a list of behaviors—sexual and non-sexual alike: sexual sin, greed, drunkenness, adultery, slander, idolatry, exploitation (1 Cor. 6:9–10).

But here's what we sometimes miss: *That list is not a verdict—it's a diagnosis.* It isn't describing people whom God is eager to condemn. *It's describing the condition of those who have not yet turned to Christ.* It describes humanity *without Christ*, not the destiny of someone who turns to Him.

And truthfully, the final judgment of any person is outside my jurisdiction. It isn't my place to declare someone "in" or "out," and that isn't the point I'd lead with anyway.

What I *do* know is this: We are living in a season of mercy, a window in which God is patiently calling all of us to Himself (2 Pet. 3:9). Yes, judgment will come, but right now the invitation of Jesus is not centered around damnation—it is centered around *grace*.

So let me answer your question directly: Hell is not for "gay people." Hell is for anyone, straight or gay, who ultimately rejects the grace, love, and lordship of Jesus and chooses a life apart from Him (Matt. 25:41; John 3:18–19).

And here's one thing I do know: *When Jesus calls anyone to follow Him, He calls every one of them to lay down anything that competes with His leadership in their lives* (Luke 9:23).

Every disciple has desires they must surrender. Every disciple has a cross to carry. Every disciple has places God lovingly confronts and reshapes.

Following Jesus isn't about starting with hell. It's about starting with *lordship*, *grace*, *surrender*, and *transformation*—trusting Him enough to align our lives with His design, even when it requires sacrifice.

KEYS FOR THE CONVERSATION

Every chapter has a lot of moving pieces, but if you can remember these keys, you'll carry the heart of this chapter and the tools you'll need into every conversation.

1. What You Need to Know

Boldness isn't bravado. It's not volume, aggression, or shock value. Biblical boldness is clarity with conviction.

Our generation is drawn to strong voices. This is why it's important to be bold: Boldness rooted in Christ cuts through the noise without cutting people down.

2. What You Need to Do

Don't shrink back when the moment calls for clarity.

Don't hide behind vague, safe, or overly polished language when truth needs to be said plainly.

3. Who You Need to Become

Become the kind of person whose courage is tempered with grace—not recklessness. Someone whose confidence is shaped by time with Jesus, not by the culture's appetite for outrage.

Chapter 7

HOLIER THAN THOU?

The credibility of the gospel is inseparable from the visible love of Christians for one another.

Francis A. Schaeffer

The Distinctiveness of Your Life Is the First Apologetic

Paul once said to the Corinthians, "You yourselves are our letter, written on our hearts, known and read by everyone. You show that you are a letter from Christ ... written not with ink but with the Spirit of the living God" (2 Cor. 3:2–3 NIV). In other words, before people ever pick up a Bible, they read *you*. Your life is a living epistle—an open letter about the reality of Jesus.

Jesus echoed this: "Let your light shine before others, so that they may see your good works and give glory to your Father who is in heaven" (Matt. 5:16 ESV). Paul taught that, in a crooked generation, believers should "shine among them like stars in the sky" (Phil. 2:15 NIV). Peter urged his readers: "Keep your conduct among the Gentiles honorable, so that when they speak against you as evildoers, they may see your good deeds and glorify God" (1 Pet. 2:12 ESV).

Before you ever explain a verse, build a case for God, or argue for the resurrection, your life is already saying something about who He is or isn't to you. Peter doesn't start his famous "gentleness and respect" line with "Always be ready to give a defense." He begins with "Sanctify the Lord God in your hearts" (1 Pet. 3:15).

That word *sanctify* means "to make holy" or "to set apart."[1] It's the language of worship. Before your words can defend the hope that is within you, your life must demonstrate that Christ is the one you fear, obey, and love above all else. When Christ is set apart (sanctified) in your heart, the outworking is a life that is itself set apart, a life that cannot help but look different from the culture around it.

Before people ever pick up a Bible, they read *you*. Your life is a living epistle—an open letter about the reality of Jesus.

Do you see the pattern? Over and over, Scripture reminds us that our lives are the first witness. That's what I mean when I say the distinctiveness of your life is the first apologetic. This means that before they hear what you say, they will see how you live. If they do believe what you say, it will be based on what they see in your life.

In a recent interview, a young woman made a striking claim: "Men need a masculine God—one they fear."[2] She wasn't alone in this thought. With the confidence of cultural observation, she suggested that Islam was better suited for men because it inflicts a certain level of fear and order. By contrast, she claimed Christianity doesn't really "work" for men. In her words, Christianity lets people just "do whatever you want, say a prayer before you die, and go to heaven."

She framed Christianity as soft. Easy. Flimsy.

And that's a sentiment more and more people seem to share. Islam is painted as strict, disciplined, ruled by law, and thus a faith for the strong. Christianity—grace-filled, forgiving, rich in mercy—is mocked as a faith for the weak or lazy. One makes demands. The other seems to give free passes.

This, of course, is not true. But perceptions have power.

In our culture, Christianity is often treated casually, even flippantly. Not long ago, there was a show on Adult Swim where Jesus, played by a Black man in sneakers, walked the streets of LA like a character out of the movie *Friday* and smoked weed on a stoop. At Pride parades, people have dressed as a queer Jesus in glitter on a cross. A decade or so ago, the "Jesus is my homeboy" trend swept pop culture, reducing the Savior of the world into a slogan for T-shirts and mugs. And to this day, Jesus' name gets used as a punchline, attached to agendas, or tossed around casually in jokes.

These aren't mere mischaracterizations. They are caricatures drawn with bold lines and repeated so often they become recognizable, even familiar. And they appear in every generation. Jesus becomes whoever people want Him to be—anything but Lord.

Meanwhile, Islam is respected, or at least feared. Men pray five times a day, publicly. They recite Arabic. They fast with intensity. There are strict codes of modesty and behavior. There are rules ... and consequences. And almost never do we see anyone parody the prophet Muhammad. I don't think in my lifetime I've ever heard his name used in vain or seen an *SNL* sketch mocking him or a sitcom reducing his authority to a punchline. To many, the very idea feels off-limits, dangerous, even unthinkable.

And I get it. I understand why it feels that way.

Islam does carry a visible seriousness. There's a rigidity, a weightiness, a structure to it that, on the surface, seems more demanding than the casual way Christianity is often practiced in the West. It's not hard to understand why someone might assume that Islam is "harder" and therefore "stronger."

But the strength of a faith system isn't measured by the severity of its rules. Nor is discipline exclusive to Islam. The truth is, Christianity calls its followers to a holy kind of hardness too. Jesus doesn't call us to casual faith. He calls us to carry a cross. To deny ourselves. To die daily. The Christian life isn't soft; it's sacrificial. And the Bible does not shy away from metaphors to make that clear.

- For example, Christians are called soldiers. "Endure hardship as a good soldier of Jesus Christ," Paul writes in 2 Timothy 2:3.
- Christians are also called athletes. In 1 Corinthians 9:24–26, Paul describes the believer as one who trains, disciplines, and runs in such a way as to win the prize.
- Paul describes the Christian life as spiritual warfare. In Ephesians 6:10–17, he urges believers to put on the armor of truth and righteousness, the gospel of peace, the shield of faith, the helmet of salvation, the sword of the Spirit. This isn't the imagery of a soft religion. This is the call to stand in battle.

- And Christians are called to be living sacrifices. "Present your bodies as a living sacrifice, holy and acceptable to God, which is your spiritual worship" (Rom. 12:1 ESV). Jesus Himself said, "If anyone desires to come after Me, let him deny himself, and take up his cross, and follow Me" (Matt. 16:24).

I'll never forget something that Tom Terrance, one of my professors at Oxford, said in class: "The thing about being a living sacrifice is that you can always get off the altar." The air in the room shifted when he said it. That's the struggle—daily consecration. Staying on the altar. Staying surrendered.

In other words, holiness isn't automatic. It's cultivated, but it's essential, because the credibility of your witness is your first defense.

That's not new. God's people have always been marked, not by how much they fit in with society, but by how clearly they stood apart from it. The metaphors may shift—soldiers, athletes, living sacrifices—but the calling is the same: to be set apart. From the very beginning, the people of God have been uniquely carved out to sanctify Him and be sanctified. This has always been the mark of His people: consecrated, distinct, and different.

And nowhere is that clearer than in the story of Israel.

Their distinctiveness was fascinating. God didn't give them rules randomly or to keep them busy; He wired their whole way of life to be a walking argument about who He is. Their life itself was their defense.

Over and over again, God told His people to avoid the customs of the surrounding nations.

> You shall not do as they do in the land of Egypt, where you lived, and you shall not do as they do in the land of Canaan, to which I am bringing you. You shall not walk in their statutes. You shall follow my rules and keep my statutes and walk in them. I am the LORD your God. (Lev. 18:3–4 ESV)

Take their diet. The laws regarding clean and unclean food weren't about nutrition (Lev. 11). They were about creating daily habits that made Israel bump up against their neighbors and say, "We're different because we belong to Yahweh." Even clothing and agriculture laws (like not mixing fabrics or seeds; Lev. 19:19 and Deut. 22:11) were constant reminders: "Don't blend in. Don't confuse covenant identity with mere cultural practice."

That same principle helps us understand other laws that often get pulled out of context—like the prohibition against tattoos (Lev. 19:28). In Leviticus, the issue wasn't body art in general. In pagan cultures of that region, people marked their skin to mourn the dead or summon their gods. God's people weren't to wear idolatry on their bodies. Same with shaving heads or cutting beards: Those were tied to pagan rituals. Circumcision was another distinction, a marker to signify, "I belong to Yahweh."

That same distinction shaped Israel's worship. Ancient cities were filled with temples, each one containing an idol as an effort to localize and control a god. Israel's temple stood apart. It held no image, only the ark and the mercy seat, an empty throne declaring that the living God cannot be carved, managed, or reduced. He meets His people by His presence, not by possession.

Even Israel's sacrifices reflected this difference. While other nations offered sacrifices to feed or manipulate their gods, Israel's sacrifices were centered on atonement, covenant faithfulness, and transformation.

God didn't need food. He wanted justice, mercy, and holiness.

Put it all together: meals, bodies, clothes, temples, sacrifices, calendars, economics. It all preached. Israel's distinction was not just cultural quirk; it was theological witness. Their life argued for God.

Why? Because that difference was its own testimony. God says it plainly in Leviticus 20:26: "You shall be holy to Me, for I the LORD am holy, and have separated you from the peoples, that you should be Mine."

And it worked. Other nations noticed. People from other nations traveled to Jerusalem because of Israel's distinctiveness. For example, 1 Kings 10 tells us about the queen of Sheba making the trip because she had heard of Solomon's wisdom and God's presence with His people. Their festivals, their temple, their insistence on one God in a world of many—these things sparked questions and drew attention. Israel's distinctiveness made the surrounding world curious, even jealous, about their God (Deut. 4:6–8).

Holiness Misunderstood: Three Common Errors

No doubt about it: Israel was called to be a holy nation. But if you ask most people what holiness means, you'll probably hear something about behavior—what you do, what you don't do, or what you do or don't wear.

For centuries, believers have struggled to define what it means to be "set apart," and somewhere along the way, we confused holiness with image.

Holiness is often misunderstood in three main ways:

1. Holiness as isolation
2. Holiness as performance
3. Holiness as external avoidance

Let's walk through each one.

Holiness Is Not Isolation

Throughout history, people have mistaken holiness for withdrawal. The instinct is understandable: The world feels corrupt, and separation feels safe. What does "set apart" mean but being placed in some spot away from the rest? The Essenes in ancient Judaism thought so too; they retreated into the desert, convinced that purity could be preserved through distance. Later, the monastic movements of the Middle Ages followed a similar path, building secluded communities devoted to prayer and simplicity.

Holiness isn't about hiding. It's about being present without being polluted. True sanctity shines brightest in the middle of life, not outside of it.

Now, to be fair, it did work to a degree. Some of those monastics preserved truth for future generations. We wouldn't have the Dead Sea Scrolls without the Essenes, for example. Their devotion wasn't wasted.

But even the purest retreat can drift into the illusion that proximity equals compromise; that to be holy, you must be absent.

That's not the model Jesus gave us. He didn't avoid life; He entered it. He attended weddings, shared meals, and sat with sinners. Not to mention the fact that He donned a robe of human flesh as the ultimate act of nonavoidance. His holiness wasn't about escaping the world but redeeming it. He withdrew only long enough to pray, then came right back down the mountain into the mess of human need.

So holiness isn't about hiding. It's about being present without being polluted. True sanctity shines brightest in the middle of life, not outside of it.

Holiness Is Not Performance

Then there's performance, the belief that holiness is about doing everything right. That's where the Pharisees got it wrong. They put on the externals of holiness but missed its substance. They perfected the posture of righteousness, the sound of prayer, and the outward appearance of devotion. But Jesus said their righteousness was superficial—it didn't reach the heart.

Paul later echoed this when he warned Timothy about those who have "a form of godliness" but deny its power (2 Tim. 3:5). The power he's referring to is the transforming presence of God, the only thing that makes holiness real.

Jesus told His followers, "Unless your righteousness exceeds that of the scribes and Pharisees, you will never enter the kingdom of heaven" (Matt. 5:20 ESV). That statement would've shocked them. The Pharisees were the gold standard of rule keeping. If they were barred from the kingdom of heaven, then who could get in? But Jesus wasn't calling for more rule following; He was calling for a different kind of righteousness; a righteousness that doesn't originate from human effort but from divine grace.

This is what Martin Luther called a foreign righteousness[3]—the righteousness of Christ that is imputed to us, not earned by us. That's why Jesus said, "Blessed are those who hunger and thirst for righteousness, for they shall be filled" (Matt. 5:6). Holiness doesn't come from striving harder; it comes from staying closer to Him.

Holiness Is Not About External Avoidance

Finally, holiness is not about avoiding the world's trappings; it's about resisting the world's *values*.

We've all seen versions of external holiness. In some church traditions, it looked like strict dress codes for women such as no pants, no jewelry, no makeup. In others, it was the expectation that men would always wear suits, or that real worship required a certain sound or look. And today, we debate whether praise leaders should wear ripped jeans.

I remember one Sunday when I was sitting behind a drum kit—because, yes, I'm a drummer—playing for a choir. After the final song, the guest preacher stepped to the pulpit. Instead of beginning his message, he turned around, pointed directly at me, and used my outfit as a public example of how the house of God was being disrespected.

I was wearing jeans and a Philadelphia Eagles T-shirt.

What followed was a publicly humiliating, five-minute rant about how it's not about being cool; it's about being holy. As you can imagine, I walked out angry—not because I was embarrassed, but because something deeper felt wrong. It felt less like pastoral care and more like a power move.

And what the man didn't know was that my faith was already fragile. I was wrestling with doubts and struggling internally, and that moment didn't help. He didn't know my story. He didn't know what I was carrying. He didn't know if that was all I owned or if I was brand-new to the faith. And that's the danger of confusing external conformity with true holiness: You can correct appearances while crushing people.

Now, modesty and reverence are still important. Scripture teaches both. But none of those external things make us holy. You can wear a suit and be carnal. You can wear sneakers and be sanctified.

Worldliness isn't about clothing; it's about cravings. John wrote, "Do not love the world or the things in the world.... For all that is in the world—the lust of the flesh, the lust of the eyes, and the pride of life—is not of the Father but is of the world" (1 John 2:15–16).

That's not about material possessions; it's about misplaced affection. When our love for the world exceeds our love for God, that's worldliness. When Paul said that Demas "loved this present world" (2 Tim. 4:10), he wasn't talking about parties or possessions, he was talking about a heart that had drifted from devotion.

Even the verse telling Christians to "come out from among them" (2 Cor. 6:17) wasn't about isolation ... it was about allegiance. Paul was warning believers against idolatry (1 Cor. 5:9–10), not engagement.

That's why we have to be careful with how we define what's "worldly." Some believers, for instance, point to Jeremiah 10:3–4 as proof that putting up a Christmas tree is pagan. But context matters.

Jeremiah wasn't describing a holiday tradition; he was condemning idol worship—trees carved into images and covered in gold, worshipped as gods. The problem wasn't decoration but deification.

The same goes for debates around holidays like Christmas, Easter, or Halloween. I'm not here to give a dissertation on any of those, but I will say that celebrating them the way our culture does doesn't automatically make you unholy. Putting up a tree, painting eggs, or dressing your kids up as superheroes for candy doesn't make you worldly.

You can't measure holiness by what you abstain from. Paul warned against the mindset that says, "Do not handle! Do not taste! Do not touch!" He said such rules have "an appearance of wisdom" but lack any power to actually restrain sin (Col. 2:21–23 NIV).

Holiness is not about living by restriction; it's about living by relationship.

When Jesus prayed, "Sanctify them by Your truth. Your word is truth" (John 17:17), He was defining holiness as alignment with God, not separation from life. It's not about distance, performance, or behavior modification. It's about proximity, presence, and transformation.

Holiness is not how far you stay from the world; it's how close you stay to Him.

It's important to hold this tension well. On one hand, yes, God absolutely gave His people visible distinctions. They were dietary, ritual, and moral boundaries designed to reveal something about His character and to form Israel into a people set apart for His purpose. The visible markers mattered because God was doing something unique in redemptive history. They weren't arbitrary rules; they were prophetic symbols pointing forward to the holiness that would one day be written on human hearts.

Holiness is not about living by restriction; it's about living by relationship.

But those visible signs were never meant to replace the inner life. They were meant to reveal it. The externals had meaning only insofar as they flowed from something deeper. The moment they became detached from the heart, they turned into hollow formalism—rituals without relationship.

So yes, the visible still matters, but only when it's animated by the invisible.

That's why Paul was constantly reminding the early church that holiness wasn't theoretical but had to take shape in real, visible obedience. He told the Corinthians to stop suing one another in public courts, for example. He told them to flee sexual immorality, to discipline arrogance, and to restore unity. Don't complain before pagan judges. Don't tolerate sexual sin. Don't flaunt gifts in arrogance. Don't divide into cliques. All of that would blur the witness of the church. Paul's message was consistent: Your credibility is your defense.

In other words, visible holiness has weight, but only when it grows out of internal transformation. Otherwise, it's just behavior management dressed up as spirituality.

So, if sanctifying Christ in your heart leads to a sanctified life, then understanding what that means couldn't be more vital. Because if a holy life is the first apologetic, if the distinctiveness of our lives is the first message people read about who God is, then we have to be clear about what holiness truly is.

When Christ sanctifies the heart, holiness becomes visible in the life. And when holiness takes root in the life, the gospel becomes tangible before we ever say a word.

Distinction and Enemy Love

For Israel, it was circumcision and diets that marked them as different from surrounding cultures. For the New Testament church, the first public marker was *baptism*. Because the new covenant places less emphasis on external markers, many tend to think that the New Testament gets away from the sacredness of the Old Testament. But Christ's new covenant doesn't erase that call to distinction; it deepens it.

The difference is that the disciples were not set apart because they kept a kosher diet or wore certain fabrics. They were marked by something even stranger: love. And not just love for God or neighbor (because every Jew already knew those commands), but love for their enemies (Matt. 5:43–44).

That was a new kind of holy—a radical, countercultural way of living that made the world stop and stare.

You didn't slip into the Christian faith quietly. There were markers that signaled belonging. Under the old framework, circumcision marked someone as being part of God's people. Later, baptism served as a visible line in the sand. It said, "I belong to Jesus." Those signs mattered. They still do. They publicly declare allegiance and draw clear lines of identity.

But as important as those markers were, something in this new way of life spoke even more loudly than any ritual ever could.

Enemy love.

Christian love for enemies was one of the most radical distinctions Jesus ever introduced. It was foreign to everyone listening. The Jews already knew "love the LORD your God" and "love your neighbor as yourself" (Mark 12:30–31). That wasn't new. But when Jesus taught that His followers should love their *enemies* and pray for those who persecuted them (Matt. 5:44), it disrupted everything they thought they understood about righteousness. That was something new—a radical commitment that no law, tradition, or philosophy had ever produced.

Today, though, we've heard it so many times that the strangeness of it barely registers. "Love your enemies" rolls off the tongue, but it's one of the most unnatural things a human being could ever do. Just look at the world we live in, how much energy we spend hating one another. From global conflict and civil war to street violence, gang rivalries, and the cattiness of reality TV, it's all fueled by offense and ego. Our political climate is toxic with contempt. Our online comment sections are battlefields. Racial division still runs deep.

Even in pop culture, hatred has become an art form. When Kendrick Lamar took shots at Drake, it wasn't surface-level disagreement. He made it painstakingly clear his disdain went beyond actions. Criticizing Drake's demeanor, down to the smallest details of how he carried himself and how he spoke, wasn't merely lyrical sparring; it was venom disguised as entertainment.[4] We consume animosity as if it's normal. But Jesus' words cut against that grain completely.

And hatred is not just "out there" in the world. It's in us too. Think about your own life. The people who've hurt you. The ones who betrayed you. The moments you replay in your head. We all know the sting of resentment and the pull toward retaliation. Loving your enemy isn't just hard; it feels impossible.

Yet as difficult as it may be, Jesus said, "You have heard that it was said, 'An eye for an eye and a tooth for a tooth.' But I tell you ..." (Matt. 5:38–39). In other words, "I know what you've been taught—what's been normalized by culture, conditioned by upbringing, and passed down through generations—but I'm calling you higher."

He wasn't just challenging behavior; He was confronting nature. He knew how much of a roadblock this would be. That's why He spent so much time stressing this to His disciples, because enemy love isn't learned in theory; it's forged in tension. It's one thing to read it. It's another thing to live it.

This is what the Pharisees got wrong, and we often do too. They thought holiness was about separation, precision, appearances, and purity of image. They had mastered the mechanics of holiness. They knew the Scriptures, memorized the prayers, tithed meticulously, and kept every actionable command. In a culture that equated external precision with internal devotion, they looked flawless. To the casual observer, they were the model of righteousness.

But Jesus wasn't impressed. Jesus revealed that true holiness is measured by the capacity to love. Over and over, He challenged their assumption that outward performance was proof of inward purity. Theirs was a holiness of optics—measured by posture, tone, and ritual—but not by love. And that's the very thing the prophets had rebuked the people for over the centuries. Isaiah cried out, "These people come near to me with their mouth and honor me with their lips, but their hearts are far from me" (Isa. 29:13 NIV). It wasn't a new problem; it was an old one dressed in new robes.

So when the disciples asked Jesus about the law, it wasn't a random theological question ... it was a sincere search for clarity. They were surrounded by religious professionals who looked holy but lacked compassion, and they wanted to know: What does God really require?

By the time Jesus arrived on the scene, the law of Moses had been expanded far beyond the Ten Commandments. Through generations of rabbinic interpretation, the 10 had multiplied into 613 laws, moral, ceremonial, and civil, plus a complex web of oral traditions designed to keep people from coming close to breaking the laws.[5] The intention may have been protection, but the result was distortion. Obedience became performance. Piety became politics. Holiness became theater.

Jesus' answer simplified everything while deepening it at the same time. He said, "You shall love the LORD your God with all your heart, with all your soul, and with all your mind." Followed by, "You shall love your neighbor as yourself" (Matt. 22:37, 39). And then came the shock: "All the Law and the Prophets hang on these two commandments" (Matt. 22:40 NIV).

In that one statement, He reframed holiness not as rule keeping but as *love lived out.*

To drive the point home, He told the parable of the good Samaritan (Luke 10:30–37). A Jewish priest passes by a wounded Jewish man and keeps walking. A Levite, another Jewish religious insider, does the same. But it's a Samaritan, a non-Jew considered a religious enemy, who stops, bandages the Jewish man's wounds, and pays his expenses. It's no accident that Jesus chose a Samaritan; He was forcing His listeners to confront their prejudice. The hero of the story was the person they least expected. And when Jesus asked which one of the three passersby proved to be a neighbor (v. 36), the answer was obvious but painfully humbling: The one who showed mercy. The one who loved.

The priest and Levite represent more than first-century hypocrisy; they represent a recurring human pattern: the tendency to settle for "religion without relationship." To substitute ritual for compassion. To perform rather than to love.

Paul echoed this sentiment in his letter to the church of Corinth: "Though I speak with the tongues of men and of angels, but have not love, I have become sounding brass or a clanging cymbal" (1 Cor. 13:1). You can do all the right things, say all the right words, even make great sacrifices, and still miss the heart of God. Without love, it's just noise.

Distinction, holiness, and set-apartness ... without love, these things create sinful moral superiority. Jesus is after humility and love.

From Old Testament to New, the story is consistent: God's people are supposed to look different. And that difference is what makes the message believable.

When people lose their distinction, they lose their credibility. Blurred lines make for a blurred witness. Distinction is not about superiority. It's about clarity.

So yes, holiness matters. Distinction matters. But the mark of God's people isn't a costume; it's a Christlike life. When Jesus is sanctified in your heart, your life gives weight to the words you speak and the arguments you make.

CURIOUS CONVERSATION

A conversation with a Hebrew Israelite

In this chapter, I talked a little about some things prohibited in the Old Testament laws that uniquely applied to the children of Israel. God had given them to keep His people distinct from their pagan neighbors and set them apart in worship, lifestyle, and identity.

All the way back to the time of Jesus' apostles, there's been a debate about whether those same laws were meant for all people at all times. In other words, should Christians today still be keeping the law in the same strict way Israel did?

As I was writing, a contemporary version of that same tension came to mind: a group known as the Hebrew Israelites—or as they're sometimes called, the Black Israelites.

Now, to be clear, I'm not referring to the Ashkenazi Jews or the Orthodox Jewish community. I'm referring to those, often very militant in posture and tone, who believe that they themselves are the true descendants of ancient Israel.

Though not entirely unified, the Hebrew Israelite movement centers around two major points of emphasis: identity and morality.

For them, identity is everything. They see the Bible almost as a kind of spiritual DNA kit, using genealogies and prophecies to trace their heritage back to the Israelites of Scripture. And morality, particularly expressed through law keeping, for them is proof of that identity.

In other words, they believe salvation is directly tied to recognizing who they are as the true Israelites and to keeping the laws that were given to Israel.

Because this group is so aggressive, particularly in the way they antagonize Christians, often preaching loudly outside of megachurches on Sunday mornings as congregants are walking in, I thought it was important to take a moment to zero in on how to have a conversation with a Hebrew Israelite.

Possible Dialogue

Them—Objection

You Christians always say we're not under the law, but that's a lie. God never changed. Jesus said He didn't come to destroy the law, but to fulfill it.

You—Rude Response

Well, if keeping the law could save you, Jesus wasted His time dying on the cross.

Why This Doesn't Work

That line might sound clever, but to someone deeply rooted in Torah identity, it feels like mockery—not logic. They hear that as you dismissing obedience.

Remember, they see obedience as evidence of devotion. The moment they sense you equate law keeping with legalism, they shut down.

Better Response

You—Affirm

No, you're absolutely right that God never changes—He's the same yesterday, today, and forever. And Jesus did not come to destroy the law but to fulfill it. On that, we completely agree. We're on the same page there.

Empathize

And I'll be honest—putting all of these passages together, trying to reconcile the law and grace, the Old Covenant and the New, can be complex. None of this is simple. These are deep theological questions that require real wrestling, and I respect anyone who's trying to make sense of how all this fits together.

Ask

When we highlight passages about grace, redemption, and forgiveness through Christ—and we talk about how we understand the role of the law—what exactly do you hear us saying?

Do you hear us minimizing the law? Do you hear us devaluing obedience?

Is it possible that we're saying something deeper about how law and grace actually work together?

Answer

First, let me acknowledge again how important the law is. As Christians, we sometimes lose sight of that in conversation, but we absolutely understand that "the law is holy, and the commandment holy and just and good" (Rom. 7:12).

In fact, this is one thing we Christians share in common with devout Hebrew Israelites: a deep reverence for the law of God and a sense of responsibility to obey His commands (Ps. 19:7; Rom. 7:12).

So where do the roads divide?

As much as we acknowledge the sacredness of the law, we also understand its limitations. When God gave Israel the law, He gave a sacrificial system alongside it. The question is why?

Because He knew they would never be able to keep the law perfectly. The sacrificial system existed to provide atonement—so that when the law was inevitably broken, sin could still be forgiven (Lev. 17:11; Heb. 9:6–10). The very existence of the sacrifices was evidence that the law, while holy, could not save by itself (Rom. 3:20).

And it's precisely here that God promised to do what the law could never do—to give His people a new heart that could truly love and obey Him from within (Jer. 31:31–34).

That leads to the unavoidable question: If the law required sacrifice for forgiveness, and those sacrifices had to be offered continually, what do you do now that there is no temple?

What happens when there is no priesthood, no altar, and no system for atonement?

The New Testament answers that question directly. The letter to the Hebrews explains that the law was "a shadow of the good things to come" and that its repeated sacrifices could never fully remove sin (10:1–4). Christ, however, offered Himself once for all, accomplishing what the law pointed toward but could never complete (v. 14).

In other words, the law commands righteousness, but Christ imparts it.

Them—Rebuttal 1

But God said He would change the heart of *Israel*. Jeremiah promised a new heart for the Jews. Jesus said He came for the lost sheep of the house of Israel. Those promises aren't for everyone; they're for Israel alone.

You—Affirm

I understand that perspective. In your framework, passages like Jeremiah 31 and Ezekiel 36 are directed specifically to Israel. You hold that God's covenant promises, His favor, and even His Spirit are uniquely tied to His chosen people. And I also understand that, within your view, God's judgment toward certain nations and His love toward Israel both serve as demonstrations of His righteousness. I'm not ignoring or minimizing that; I recognize how central that distinction is to your theology and reading of Scripture.

Empathize

And honestly, I get it. When identity and history have been stripped away, it's powerful to find yourself in the biblical narrative again. To trace your lineage back to Abraham and to reclaim the law, covenantal inheritance, and the promises of God is not trivial. It carries real weight.

Ask

But can I ask you something?

If God's covenant promises were meant to stop with Israel, why do we keep seeing Him extend His mercy beyond Israel's borders—from Genesis to Revelation?

Why would God tell Abraham, "All peoples on earth will be blessed through you" (Gen. 12:3 NIV)? Why would Isaiah 19:25 record God calling Egypt "My people" and Assyria "the work of My hands"?

If His heart was for one nation only, why does He keep making room for others?

Answer

Throughout Scripture, we see that God *began* His redemptive work through Israel but always intended to expand it to all nations (Gen. 12:1–3; 18:18).

From the very beginning, God's promise to Abraham was not just about blessing one people—it was about blessing every people. Israel was chosen as the vessel, not the endpoint.

Isaiah captures it perfectly: "It is too small a thing for you ... to restore the tribes of Jacob.... I will also make you a light for the Gentiles, that my salvation may reach to the ends of the earth" (49:6 NIV).

Throughout the prophets, we see God's heart turned outward. And when we reach the New Testament, that promise begins to unfold in real time.

In the book of Acts, we see the Holy Spirit poured out first in Jerusalem and then spilling across every boundary—Judea, Samaria, and the Gentile world (Acts 1:8). The early church wrestled with this expansion, but it became clear that God was grafting the nations into His covenant family.

Paul explains this beautifully in Romans 9–11. The Gentiles, he says, have been grafted into the olive tree of God's covenant, while some branches of Israel have been temporarily cut off because of unbelief. Yet even that, Paul says, is part of God's larger plan—so that mercy can eventually be shown to everyone.

And Revelation gives us the final picture: "A great multitude which no one could number, of all nations, tribes, peoples, and tongues, standing before the throne and before the Lamb" (7:9).

This does not represent a replacement of Israel; it's the fulfillment of Israel's purpose—to be a light to the world (Isa. 60:1–3).

So yes, the new-heart promise began with Israel. But through Christ, that same Spirit of renewal is now available to all humanity (Acts 2:38–39). The covenant started with a people; it culminates in a Savior.

Them—Rebuttal 2

Okay, so you're saying the law couldn't save us, and that Christ fulfilled it. But how are you sanctified if you're not following the commandments? Doesn't the Bible say the law converts the soul?

You—Affirm

These are really valid questions; and honestly, I appreciate anyone who's asking them. You're not wrong for wanting clarity about how holiness works.

Empathize

Man, I get it. We all want to get this thing right. Nobody wants to live in a way that dishonors God. We're all just trying to figure out what obedience looks like and how to honor God.

Ask

Can I ask you something, though? When you think about sanctification—being made holy—do you see it more as something we do for God or something God does within us?

Answer

First, let me clarify something. You said, "How are you sanctified if you're not following the commandments?"

The truth is, Christians *are* following the commandments. Jesus said, "If you love Me, you'll keep My commandments" (John 14:15, 21). We believe obedience matters deeply.

But we also understand the limitations of the commandments. The law is good and righteous, but it doesn't have the power to save, transform, or renew from the inside out. It can expose sin, but it can't heal it (Rom. 7:7). It can reveal what holiness looks like, but it can't make us holy (Heb. 7:18–19).

So yes, we keep the commandments, but we do it from a different place than the Jewish people did. We obey because we've been made new, not to make ourselves new. Beyond that, we believe that Jesus embodies the law—He is its fulfillment, not its negation (Matt. 5:17; Rom. 10:4).

However, the writer of Hebrews takes it a step further. Writing to a Jewish-Christian audience, he shows that Jesus is greater than Moses (3:1–6), greater than Joshua (4:8–10), greater than the angels, greater than the high priest, greater than the sacrificial system, and greater than the blood of bulls and goats (9:11–14).

In other words, with everything the law pointed toward ... Jesus is greater (Col. 2:16–17).

So how are we sanctified? The writer of Hebrews answers that directly in 10:14: "By one offering He has perfected forever those who are being sanctified."

That's it. That's the key.

We're sanctified not through the endless striving of commandment keeping, but through the once-for-all work of Christ (10:10). His Spirit continues that process in us day by day—shaping us, correcting us, and conforming us to His image (Rom. 8:29).

Our obedience is not the source of our holiness; it flows from the holiness Christ has already secured for us.

The law commands righteousness, but Christ imparts it.

So you see, we do keep the commandments. But we do so as those who've been transformed from the inside out. The law can regulate behavior, but only grace can regenerate the heart.

The law shows us what holiness looks like; Christ makes holiness possible. I know we see this differently, but from where I stand, God's plan has always been both particular and universal—particular in that He chose Israel, and universal in that He chose Israel for the world.

The covenant began local, but grace ends global. The promise started with Israel, but it's fulfilled in Christ.

KEYS FOR THE CONVERSATION

Every chapter has a lot of moving pieces, but if you can remember these keys, you'll carry the heart of this chapter and the tools you'll need into every conversation.

1. What You Need to Know

Self-righteousness doesn't usually show up loud; it shows up subtle. It's the quiet drift toward believing your spiritual maturity makes you morally superior. *Remember that holiness never gives you height to look down on someone; it gives you depth to kneel beside them.*

2. What You Need to Do

Practice treating sin as a *humanity-wide* problem. Not as "your sin" but as "our sin." Never shrink back from speaking the truth, but always refuse to weaponize it.

3. Who You Need to Become

Become someone who refuses to use holiness as a hammer but allows it to be a light—one that exposes without humiliation or shame. Strive to live a life characterized by humility.

Chapter 8

BUT NOBODY ASKED YOU

Do not try to be everything to everyone. Let your presence speak even when your mouth is closed.

Attributed to Saint Francis of Assisi

Have you ever been in a conversation with someone, only for a third party to overhear and suddenly insert themselves in the discussion? Unsolicited and uninvited, they jump in with their opinions.

They might start in with a line like, "I couldn't help but overhear you guys talking, but here's what I think ..." Before you know it, they've monopolized the conversation while you and the other person stand there listening.

You probably wouldn't say this out loud, but if you're like me, in your head you're probably thinking: *Firstly, who is this person? And secondly, thank you for your opinion, but nobody asked for it.*

I know that might come off as mean (and rude!), but it's the truth. We've all experienced moments like this. In fact, I must confess, there was a time in my life when I was that intrusive person.

I felt responsible for fixing everyone else's theology. Not just by teaching on a stage or guiding those who sought me out for advice. Nope. Instead, I actively got involved in policing doctrine wherever I went, like I'd been divinely appointed as the guardian of all things biblical. I know; it's terrible, right? And I'm sorry!

I've spent a good portion of my life walking alongside high-profile people, counseling, answering theological questions, and helping bring clarity to Scripture. And I've always found fulfillment in that call. As Paul put it, it makes my joy complete (Phil. 2:2). I love pouring into people, helping them see truth, clearing up misconceptions, and strengthening their faith.

But somewhere along the way, I crossed a line.

People Aren't Projects

Instead of staying in my lane and ministering to those who asked for my advice, I started to feel that it was my duty to correct bad theology wherever I saw it. And when you think it's your duty, you don't wait for an invitation. You step in uninvited. Always on a mission.

I wasn't getting to know people authentically for the sake of a human relationship. Sometimes, I got to know them purely for the sake of gaining an opportunity to correct them.

People are not projects. They are not assignments. They are not spiritual remodels waiting for your expert opinion.

More of my interactions were guided by that agenda than I care to admit. I didn't always listen to others in order to understand. Instead,

I listened for the gap, the flaw, and the moment when I could step in and "fix" things.

And here's the hard (and brutal) truth I had to face: I wasn't just driven by passion for truth; I was driven by how I viewed people. People became projects.

And that is wrong. When we see people as projects, we reduce them to their church attendance, lifestyle choices, political views, or broken theology.

And when we do that, we stop seeing them. We come to see only what we think needs to be changed or improved. But people are not projects. They are not assignments. They are not spiritual remodels waiting for your expert opinion.

They are people with stories full of real pain, layered with complexity and (most importantly) human dignity. I want to share a quick story to illustrate what I'm talking about here.

One year, I went on an eighty-five-city tour with Christian artist Kirk Franklin. In the middle of that incredible series of events, I challenged one of the groups on the tour with us about some of their lyrics. I had concerns and believed it was my responsibility to speak up. So I did what I thought was the righteous thing to do: I confronted them in their dressing room. Understandably, the conversation was tense.

Afterward, I went back to my own space, but I could hear them talking about me through the wall.

"He's just too deep," I heard one of them say.

At the time, I took their comments as a badge of honor, as persecution for righteousness' sake. *They just don't get it*, I told myself. *They aren't serious about sound doctrine.* But life and hindsight have a way of humbling you.

Looking back, I realize they weren't rejecting the truth. They were (rightly) rejecting the fact that I had forced myself into a space that wasn't mine to fill. Nobody asked me.

Just Enjoy the Cookout

At some point, I had to ask myself the question: *Why can't you just enjoy the cookout?* Hang with me here, and this will make sense.

Family gatherings and holidays can be contentious times of the year. Some of the most awkward and tense moments can happen at the Thanksgiving dinner table. Sometimes these moments are due to personal issues, and other times the tension flares up around discussions of politics, sports, or, you guessed it, religion.

Sometimes you go looking for the fight. Go on and admit it. You've been waiting all year to use that ammunition you've been loading from the stack of theological books you've read. You're prepped and ready.

But instead of heading into the family get-together on July 4 or even Thanksgiving dinner like you're walking up to the pulpit, what if you went to enjoy the cookout? What if you went with the intent to serve and enjoy, not to spar or lecture? Not to win?

I know, your cousin is a Muslim, and your nephew still sells drugs. But maybe, just maybe, this family gathering is not the time.

Jesus' Posture: Presence Over Performance

The Bible says that Jesus ate with tax collectors and sinners (Matt. 9:11; Mark 2:16; Luke 5:30). It's one of the most commonly used sayings to highlight the importance of not separating ourselves or thinking too highly of ourselves. It's also used to affirm the importance of engaging with the world and being present where brokenness lives.

Notice, the Bible doesn't say simply that He *ate* with these tax collectors and sinners; it says He was *reclining at the table with them* (Luke 7:36; John 13:23). In Jewish culture, that's a powerful image. Reclining wasn't how you sat for a quick meal. It was how you dined when you were relaxed, when you were with people you were at home with. It meant fellowship. It meant relationship. It meant safety.[1]

So when Jesus reclined at the table with tax collectors and sinners, He wasn't just "around" them—He was *among* them. At ease. And yet He was so without compromising a single ounce of holiness. That posture signifies deep comfort and human connection. When He reclined at the table, He wasn't in debate mode. He wasn't on defense, much less offense. He was just ... present. Right at home. And yet still fully righteous.

This is part of what made the moment so beautiful.

As I sat with that picture of Jesus, the question that came to mind was simple but powerful: What was Jesus talking about in that moment?

The Bible is silent on that point. And maybe that means we should be silent on it too. Because what if it wasn't a heavy conversation but rather just dinner with friends? What if Jesus was merely enjoying a meal? What if He was simply being present?

Reading that story reminded me of another moment in Scripture that gives us a similar glimpse into the humanity and presence of Jesus.

It's the wedding at Cana (John 2:1–12). This wasn't a quick stop or a one-hour event. Weddings in Jewish culture lasted up to seven days. These were celebratory, communal, joyful feasts full of music, dancing, storytelling, food, and drink. It was a party.

And Jesus was there.[2] He wasn't preaching. He wasn't debating religious leaders. He wasn't correcting theology or calling out sin. He wasn't scanning the room taking inventory of whether the meat was kosher or if people were behaving righteously. He was at the party. Relaxed. Laughing. Mingling. Enjoying the moment.

Now yes, something spiritually significant happened there. He turned water into wine—the first recorded miracle of His public ministry. It was a moment of supernatural transformation, generosity, and provision. Some scholars even see echoes of millennial joy and celebration in that miracle.

But if you zoom in on the posture of Jesus, not the outcome, what you see is someone who knew how to be fully present. Someone who knew how to enjoy the moment.

Someone who knew how to be at the cookout.

Jesus' Model

Jesus, with all the wisdom, knowledge, and power that He possessed, rarely imposed Himself on others. He didn't walk around inserting Himself into every moment, correcting everyone, or demanding attention. He didn't grandstand. He didn't dominate every room He entered. He didn't treat people like projects.

He lived as fully God but also fully human, and that humanity modeled restraint, humility, and presence (Heb. 2:14; John 1:14). What's even more striking is how silent the Scriptures are about the first thirty years of His life.

Sure, we get glimpses: His birth (Luke 2:1–20), the visit from the magi (Matt. 2:1–12), His dedication at the temple (Luke 2:22–38), the escape to Egypt (Matt. 2:13–15), and that episode at age twelve when

He amazed the teachers with His understanding (Luke 2:41–47). But outside of those moments? Silence.

Some Gnostic gospels, like the Gospel of Thomas or the Gospel of Mary, try to fill in the gaps with stories of Jesus as a child performing miracles. But these accounts were never considered reliable or canonical.[3]

What we do have is one profound line in Luke: "And Jesus grew in wisdom and stature, and in favor with God and man" (2:52 NIV).

Yes, He grew in favor with the Father. But the emphasis here for me, in the context of this chapter, is that He grew in favor with man. That kind of favor doesn't come from correcting everyone or hijacking every conversation (Prov. 11:27; 3:3–4).

That kind of favor comes from being present, building relational equity, and being with people. Before He performed a single miracle, before He preached, before He healed, taught, or called disciples, Jesus grew, learned, listened, formed bonds, and built trust.

He lived the life of a typical Jewish man of His day: observing feasts (John 7:2, 10), attending synagogue (Luke 4:16), honoring His parents (Luke 2:51), and working with His hands (Mark 6:3). He had siblings, including James (Mark 6:3), and other relatives, such as John the Baptist, His cousin (Luke 1:36). He was known in His town as a carpenter (Matt. 13:55). He had a routine and neighbors.

That tells me that maybe enjoying the cookout, being present, serving, laughing with your cousins, holding babies, and washing the dishes is not wasted time (Eccl. 3:1, 13).

It's not a compromise or a missed opportunity; it's formation.

It's Christlike. We've already seen it modeled for us in the life of Jesus Himself (John 1:14). There's no need to be the loudest voice at the table, no need to win the point, and no need to hijack every moment with unsolicited advice (Prov. 17:27; James 1:19).

Here's my honest moment. I'm an evangelist and a teacher by nature (Eph. 4:11). So not discussing and debating my faith, especially at family gatherings, is extremely difficult for me. It's taken a while, but finally I've learned that sometimes faithfulness is found in restraint (Prov. 10:19).

You don't always have to bring the fire. Sometimes the best way to reflect Jesus is to sit in the moment, laugh at a dumb joke, play Uno, eat some ribs, and let people be people (Rom. 12:15).

Be present and build relational equity first, and then speak from trust (Prov. 20:5).

Instead of jumping into the conversation cold, let your life and character open the door (Matt. 5:16). Let your consistent presence earn you the right to speak (1 Pet. 2:12). Let love lead not only your conviction but also your engagement (1 Cor. 13:1–3).

Instead of, "I couldn't help overhearing, but here's where you're wrong," you could try, "Hey, I heard you say something earlier and I didn't want to intrude, but if you ever want to talk more about that, I'd love to."

Because when truth is spoken in the context of trust, respect, and loving relationship, it has a better shot at being heard (Eph. 4:15). Truth doesn't need a police force; it needs ambassadors (2 Cor. 5:20)—and ambassadors don't kick down doors; they go where they're invited.

As King Solomon wisely said: "Do not exalt yourself in the presence of the king" (Prov. 25:6). Don't speak so people will listen ... live in such a way that when you do speak, they want to hear what you have to say (Col. 4:5–6).

CURIOUS CONVERSATION

"Where are the lost books of the Bible?"

Although this chapter has been all about restraint—about how sometimes less is more—there are still moments when the opportunity to speak does present itself. And when that happens, wisdom says we should be ready to give a thoughtful answer.

In this chapter, I briefly mentioned the so-called "lost" or Gnostic gospels (such as the Gospel of Thomas and the Gospel of Mary)—a topic that comes up all the time, especially in the social media space. It's connected to one of the biggest and most scandalous claims made against Christianity today. People notice that the Catholic Bible, the Ethiopian Bible, and the Protestant Bible don't have the same number of books. Some people are merely curious about it; others are suspicious or skeptical.

Since this question keeps coming up, it's worth pausing here to zero in on how to have the conversation around the "lost books of the Bible."

Possible Dialogue

Them—Objection

Why did the early church reject the Gospel of Thomas and the Gospel of Mary? What were they trying to hide?

You—Rude Response

Sounds like you've been watching too many Dan Brown movies and bingeing conspiracy theories on social media.

Why This Doesn't Work

Beyond the fact that questions about "hidden books" are rarely just about manuscripts, this flippant response ignores deeper concerns of trust and often reinforces suspicion rather than easing it. Whether Scripture can be trusted or institutions have manipulated the truth usually lies at the heart of the conversation. Even if the objection is shaped by pop culture or internet conspiracies, sarcasm doesn't help. All it does is signal that the person's curiosity isn't worth taking seriously.

Better Response

You—Affirm

That's a fair question. And I get it: I love entertaining a good conspiracy theory!

Empathize

Honestly, I wrestled with this too. I remember seeing videos about the "missing" or "forbidden" books and asking the same question: Why would they be removed—unless they were a threat? That sent me down a whole rabbit hole of investigation.

Ask

Let me ask you this—do you really believe the Roman Catholic Church was involved in a coordinated conspiracy to hide certain truths from the public? Since the Catholic Bible and the Protestant Bible also have a different number of books, maybe the Protestant Reformers were part of a conspiracy too? Or is it possible there's a more nuanced explanation?

Answer

This is something I had to come to understand.

Most of us, including me, tend to think of the Bible as this magical book that God just whisked together from heaven and handed down in perfect condition. And because we assume that, anything that doesn't line up with that picture feels suspicious. But what I hadn't learned about yet or taken into consideration was the role of human agency: that God used people, processes, time, and controversy to shape what we now call the Bible.

That process is called *transmission*, and part of it involved a massive effort by brilliant, godly, and intellectually rigorous scholars from places like Carthage, Alexandria, and Antioch. These Christian scholars didn't randomly pick and choose what went into the Bible. They took the earliest manuscripts they had, gathered from different churches and regions, and laid them side by side. Then they asked:

- Does this text line up with the teachings of Jesus and the apostles?
- Does it affirm what we already know to be true about God's character?
- Was it widely accepted and used in worship by the early church?
- Was it written by an apostle or someone in direct contact with one?

If a book didn't meet those standards, it failed the test and didn't get included.

So again, it's not that these were "forbidden" books taken out later in some smoke-filled back room in Rome or Geneva. It's that they never made it in to begin with because they couldn't pass the criteria the early church used for identifying Scripture.

Was the process perfect? No. It was messy. It involved real people, real debates, and real discernment. But that doesn't make it corrupt. It makes it human ... and somehow, mysteriously, still divinely guided.[4]

Them—Rebuttal 1

But the Gospels weren't even written by the disciples. They're anonymous. We don't have the original manuscripts. We don't know who wrote what we have, and some of the writers weren't even apostles. Why would we trust anything they say?

You—Affirm

I get it. When I was told that the sources were anonymous, I had questions too. It made me curious, especially in a world full of misinformation and agendas.

Empathize

Honestly, I used to wonder about the anonymity too. Why didn't the Gospel writers just sign their names? That felt strange to me too until I started studying it for myself.

Ask

Does the fact that they didn't sign their books or explicitly identify themselves mean that we can't know who wrote them?

Answer

This objection comes from the fact that the original manuscripts of the Gospels didn't start with a byline like: "Hi, I'm Matthew, and I wrote this." But that wasn't abnormal for the time. Most ancient texts didn't work that way. That doesn't mean we're in the dark, though.

If we're being fair, there are sources outside the Bible that we trust indiscriminately—even though they too are historical accounts from anonymous or semi-anonymous sources. For instance:

- Julius Caesar's life was recorded by Roman historians like Suetonius and Plutarch, neither of whom were Caesar's close friends or eyewitnesses. Yet nobody dismisses their work (much less that Julius Caesar ever existed) on the basis of authorship.
- Homer's *Iliad* and *Odyssey* have deeply shaped Western literature and history, even though scholars still debate whether "Homer" was a single person or a collective name.[5]

So if we're being consistent, we have to say that anonymity doesn't mean inaccuracy. It just means we have to look at how the early community received and preserved those writings.[6]

Which leads to the second part of your question, that not all the Gospel writers were apostles. That's true. Mark and Luke weren't part of the original Twelve. But here's why their accounts were still trusted: proximity.

Think of it like this: If Kelly Rowland wrote a biography of Beyoncé, most people wouldn't question whether it was legit. Why? Because the two are close. Kelly was there when it happened. She grew up with her, toured with her, knew her personally.

That's what we see in the Gospels:

- Mark (also called John Mark) traveled and ministered with Peter; in fact, his Gospel is widely considered "Peter's account through Mark's pen."[7]
- Luke was a companion of Paul (Philem. 1:23–24); Luke himself was a respected historian who interviewed eyewitnesses and carefully investigated everything "from the beginning" (Luke 1:1–4).
- Matthew and John were apostles, direct eyewitnesses of the life, death, and resurrection of Jesus.

These weren't random authors writing fan fiction. These people either were eyewitnesses or deeply connected to eyewitnesses.[8]

The early church knew this.

Christians who lived in the first and second centuries consistently affirmed the authorship of Matthew, Mark, Luke, and John. They weren't speculating—they were close to the action and connected to the apostles, and they had access to firsthand witnesses. Their consensus wasn't based on blind faith; it was rooted in relationship, evidence, and proximity.

While the process might seem strange to modern eyes, it wasn't sloppy, random, or dishonest. It was deeply embedded in the early Christian community's lived experience and reverence for the truth.

Them—Rebuttal 2

What about books like Enoch, Maccabees, or the Book of the Wars of the Lord? They're mentioned, alluded to, or even quoted in the Bible—so why aren't they in the Protestant Bible?

You—Affirm

It's a valid question. If the Bible mentions certain books by name—or even quotes from them—it's not unreasonable to wonder why those books didn't make the final cut.

Empathize

Honestly, I had this exact question when I first heard that the Bible refers to other books. It felt like I had just discovered "hidden files" on God's hard drive. I wondered if we were missing out on something God wanted us to have, or even if someone had intentionally kept those books out.

Ask

Let me ask you this: Do you think every book that's referenced in another book should be treated as equal in authority or included in the same collection?

Answer

Not everything mentioned in the Bible was meant to be Scripture.

The Bible is full of references to other writings, cultural sayings, and historical documents. For example:

- The Book of Jasher is mentioned in Joshua 10:13.
- The Book of the Wars of the Lord is mentioned in Numbers 21:14.
- Paul quoted pagan poets like Aratus and Epimenides in Acts 17:28 and Titus 1:12.[9]
- Even Jude, the brother of Jesus, quotes nonbiblical books when they served his point (Jude 1:14–15). But quoting a book isn't the same as endorsing it as inspired Scripture. It means that particular part was useful to make a point.

Now, I get the tension. And you're not the first to feel it. This is actually an age-old concern. Even Martin Luther, the great Reformer, wrestled with it.

Instead of tossing out the apocryphal books completely, Luther moved seven of them (along with parts of Esther and Daniel) to the back of the Bible as a kind of addendum. Why? Because he still saw their worth. He recognized that they carried value, especially in terms of Jewish history, moral reflection, and theological insight. He just didn't believe they rose to the level of divinely inspired Scripture.

And honestly? I agree with him.

Books like Enoch, for example, contain ideas that are intriguing and that, in some cases, seem to align with other scriptures. One of the most commonly discussed doctrines that the book of Enoch derives from the scriptures and expands upon is the idea that "the sons of God" slept with the "daughters of men," and from that union came the Nephilim (Gen. 6:1–4). That interpretation (fallen angels + human women) finds some resonance in places like 1 Peter 3:18–20; 2 Peter 2:4–5; and Jude 1:6–7 and 14–15.

I'm not trying to discredit or dismiss these books. I think they do have value as historical sources, theological reflection, and background reading to help us understand the biblical world. But ...

They just don't carry the same weight.

These referenced books might be helpful, but they weren't seen as God-breathed in the same way. While they're worth reading, they're not meant for doctrine (Gal. 1:8). Think of them more like bonus material—good, even insightful at times, but not binding.

KEYS FOR THE CONVERSATION

Every chapter has a lot of moving pieces, but if you can remember these keys, you'll carry the heart of this chapter and the tools you'll need into every conversation.

1. What You Need to Know

Unsolicited advice can feel intrusive, and because of that, it can backfire. People are *less inclined* to receive truth if they feel forced, cornered, or corrected without consent. Lots of conversations collapse—not because the truth was wrong but because the timing was.

2. What You Need to Do

Resist the urge to jump in before you're invited.

Pay attention to whether a person actually wants input, clarity, correction, or counsel. If you feel compelled to weigh in, lead with questions to get a sense of how open they are to you speaking into the moment.

3. Who You Need to Become

Become someone who is secure enough to wait, patient enough to listen, and wise enough to know when—or *if*—your voice is needed.

Let your restraint communicate respect.

Chapter 9

I DON'T LIKE WHEN I'M NOT RIGHT

It is not bigotry to be certain we are right; but it is bigotry to be unable to imagine how we might possibly have gone wrong.

G. K. Chesterton, *The Catholic Church and Conversion*

The Posture of Rightness

Nothing shuts down a conversation faster than someone who already knows everything. You know the type. No matter what you say, whether it's a small observation or a major insight, they respond the same way: "Yeah, I know."

New information? Yeah, I know.

A different perspective? Yeah, I know.

Wisdom they didn't ask for but probably need? Yeah ... I know.

If I'm honest, that person has been me. I don't like when I'm not right.

It's not one of those obvious sins people can spot from a distance. It's subtle, hidden in posture, in tone, in how I respond when someone challenges what I believe or what I think I know. It doesn't always show up loudly, but when it does, it's usually in the middle of a conversation when something in me wants to defend, prove, or correct.

What I've come to realize is that this isn't just about truth. It's about ego.

Somewhere beneath the surface, there's a part of me that enjoys being right, that likes the sense of control that comes with clarity, confidence, and conviction. It feels good to have the sharper point, the cleaner logic, the final word. But when that feeling becomes a need, something in the heart shifts. The desire to defend truth starts looking a lot like the desire to win.

And that's where pride creeps in.

Scripture talks about posture a lot; not physical posture but the posture of the heart. In the kingdom of God, posture isn't about how you stand but how you bend. The question isn't whether we ever wrestle with pride (everyone does) but which way our heart leans when pride shows up. Is my heart bent toward humility or self-exaltation? Toward repentance or resistance? That bend determines everything.

David is a perfect picture of this. He wasn't flawless ... far from it ... but his heart was bent in the right direction. When he fell, he fell forward into repentance. When he sinned, he didn't defend himself; he returned to God and prayed, "Create in me a clean heart, O God, and renew a steadfast spirit within me" (Ps. 51:10).

That's what good posture looks like in the kingdom: not perfection but direction. Not never stumbling but always turning the heart back toward God. For David, part of that was his willingness to keep his sin before the Lord; to confess, to bring it into the light, to stay soft. That's what kept him close.

In the kingdom of God, posture isn't about how you stand but how you bend.

And that's what I want. Because posture determines proximity. A proud heart distances itself from grace; a humble heart draws near to grace. Proverbs 3:34 says God "mocks the mockers, but gives grace to the humble" (BSB). Even in our intellectual life—in the world of theology, debate, and apologetics—how we carry truth is as important as knowing it.

Therapy helped me see that. In one session, my therapist said something that stuck with me: "Emanuel, when you feel the need to be right, what part of you feels threatened?" That question revealed more theology than psychology. Because pride is often a defense mechanism for fear: fear of inadequacy, of being unseen, of losing control. But in the economy of grace, the way up is always down. Jesus said, "Whoever exalts himself will be humbled, and he who humbles himself will be exalted" (Matt. 23:12).

Every conversation becomes a chance to check my posture—to ask whether my heart is leaning toward self-defense or self-surrender, whether I'm standing tall in pride or bowed low in humility. Because the truth is that God does His best work in hearts that stay bent.

It's Okay to Not Know

My discomfort with being wrong is often tied to my discomfort with not knowing.

It's hard to say, "I don't know," especially when people expect you to know. But over time, I've realized that one of the healthiest, most faith-filled things I can say in a complicated conversation is exactly that: "I don't know."

That phrase used to feel like a failure. But now it feels like freedom.

Because "I don't know" isn't weakness, it's perspective. It's what keeps you grounded when conversations get complex. It reminds you that your worth isn't tied to your ability to out-argue someone; it's tied to your willingness to stay humble, honest, and teachable.

And let's be honest: These conversations are complicated. That's part of what makes this whole thing difficult. Few things are simple anymore. We live in an age of layers: emotional, historical, spiritual. People don't bring only questions; they also bring stories, wounds, experiences, and assumptions. Sometimes their question isn't really their question.

So we can't expect to have every answer. And that's okay.

There's no need to carry an unrealistic pressure to respond perfectly every time, as if one wrong answer might undo the gospel. God's truth doesn't collapse because I couldn't recall a verse or mount a defense quickly enough. Nor will God's kingdom be established on earth if I do the conversation perfectly right.

We are participants in God's work, not the architects of it.

We plant and we water, but God gives the increase (1 Cor. 3:6).

That doesn't mean we stop studying or thinking deeply—it means we stay in our lane. We remember that we are witnesses, not saviors. We play our part and open our mouths to respond, praying for His words to come out and do their work; but the rest is on God. The burden to rescue, convince, or convert doesn't belong to us. It belongs to Him.

And when that truth sinks in, we can finally rest. We can sit in the complexity without being crushed by it. We can be curious instead of controlling; present instead of pressured.

Jesus modeled this balance. When Pilate asked, "What is truth?" Jesus didn't reply (John 18:38). Not because He didn't know but because He knew when not to answer. That's not ignorance; that's discernment. Wisdom knows when to speak and when to stay silent.

If you ever find yourself in a moment when the questions outpace your understanding, take a breath. Remember: These are complex conversations.

You don't have to know everything.

You just have to be faithful with what you do know.

And that posture, that humility, is what opens the door to something powerful: listening.

Listening Is Hard

Listening sounds simple, but it's one of the hardest disciplines in the world—especially when you've already done your homework.

When you've read the books, watched the debates, and rehearsed the counterarguments, it's easy to treat conversations like chess games instead of sacred exchanges. You hear someone talking, but you're really just waiting for your turn. I know that rhythm well. I've lived it.

But over time, I've learned that listening isn't weakness. It's wisdom.

Listening creates space. It shows respect. It disarms defensiveness. It turns a battle of ideas into a bridge between hearts. And often, when you slow down long enough to really listen, you'll discover that what someone is asking isn't what they're really asking. Their tone, their story, their pain ... those things carry as much information as their words.

That's why James wrote, "Everyone should be quick to listen, slow to speak and slow to become angry" (1:19 NIV).

Jesus modeled that perfectly. He asked more questions than He answered. Not because He lacked information but because He loved revelation. He knew people often needed to hear themselves before they could hear Him.

When we listen well, we mirror Jesus. We stop fighting to be heard and start seeking to understand. We make space for grace.

Pride—The Silent Killer

At the root of so much relational breakdown, spiritual immaturity, and conversational dysfunction is one sin that rarely announces itself but always leaves wreckage behind: pride.

Not the loud, obvious kind, though that exists; but the quieter version that hides in posture, tone, and motive. The kind that turns conversations into competitions and people into obstacles. The kind that sabotages what humility could have healed.

C. S. Lewis called pride "the great sin."[1] Augustine described it as "the love of one's own excellence."[2] Paul warned Timothy not to place a new believer into leadership too quickly, "or he may become conceited and fall under the same condemnation as the devil" (1 Tim. 3:6 BSB). Pride has a long résumé, and none of it is good.

When you've read the books, watched the debates, and rehearsed the counterarguments, it's easy to treat conversations like chess games instead of sacred exchanges. You hear someone talking, but you're really just waiting for your turn.

Scripture is unflinchingly honest about where pride leads: "Pride goes before destruction, and a haughty spirit before a fall" (Prov. 16:18).

We've seen this story play out over and over again. Saul began his reign considering himself small in his own eyes (1 Sam. 15:17), but when humility gave way to self-importance, his kingdom unraveled. Nebuchadnezzar stood on his palace balcony admiring his own greatness, only to be humbled until he learned that sovereignty belongs to God alone (Dan. 4:30–37). History, biblical and otherwise, is littered with examples of people who rose quickly and fell hard because pride went unchecked.

In conversation, pride is just as destructive. It makes us defensive when we should be discerning. Loud when silence would be wiser. It pushes us to work harder when God is inviting us to rest. And instead of building bridges, pride turns connection into contention.

Humility, on the other hand, opens everything up. It softens tone, clears vision, and creates safety. Truth travels best at the pace of grace. Because the world doesn't need more *right* Christians; it needs more *real* ones.

It's too much work to carry conversations like you're the one responsible for holding everything together. It's exhausting trying to make up for—or hide—what you don't know, performing as if the outcome depends on you. Somewhere along the way, it stops being about helping others and starts being about proving yourself.

And the moment it becomes about you, the conversation loses its power.

Now, let me be clear about what I mean by *pride*, because this matters.

There is a difference between healthy confidence and being full of pride. Scripture never condemns growth, excellence, or gratitude-rooted confidence. In fact, we're encouraged to steward our gifts well, to grow in wisdom, and to work diligently before God (Matt. 25:21). Taking responsibility, pursuing excellence, and acknowledging God's work in your life is not arrogance ... it's faithfulness.

What Scripture consistently confronts is *self-exaltation*, the inward curve of the heart that places the self at the center, seeks superiority over others, and resists correction. In the context of conversation, that kind of pride shows up as the need to win, to dominate, to correct prematurely, or to be seen as the smartest person in the room. It's not confidence in God's truth; it's confidence in *self*.

I remember having a particular conversation with my oldest daughter. We were talking about hip-hop: its bravado, its swagger, its chest-thumping confidence. At one point, she asked a sincere question: "What's wrong with taking pride in yourself?" It was a fair question. Because the issue isn't confidence; it's *where that confidence is rooted*.

Confidence anchored in gratitude and dependence on God leads to humility. Confidence anchored in self-glory leads to pride. One opens doors. The other quietly closes them.

Pride kills connection.

Humility creates space.

And that's why, in conversation, humility isn't weakness; it's wisdom. It keeps the focus on the other person instead of the ego. It allows truth to be heard, not just stated. And it creates the kind of relational safety where real transformation can begin.

Because being right might end a conversation.

But being humble can open one.

CURIOUS CONVERSATION

"Why would I need to confess my sins to God?"

Possible Dialogue

Them—Objection

I don't get why I need to confess my sins to God. If He already knows everything, what's the point?

You—Rude Response

Oh, well, I don't get why you don't get it.

Why This Doesn't Work

It might sound clever, but it's dismissive. It shuts down curiosity instead of building a bridge. People ask this sincerely ... sometimes as skeptics, sometimes as seekers ... and they deserve a thoughtful answer.

Better Response

You—Affirm

Your question is spot on, and you're right that God is all-knowing. Psalm 139 says He knows our thoughts before we think them and our words before we speak them. So confession clearly isn't about informing Him of anything new.

Empathize

I think most people, even Christians, have wondered this at some point. It can feel redundant; like, why tell God what He already knows?

Ask

Have you ever tried confessing your wrongdoing to God? If so, what outcomes were you expecting? Do you feel something was missing?

Answer

Confession is not about giving God information; it's about agreement and absolution.

From the beginning, God has hardwired us to confess (Ps. 32:3–5). Something in us longs to unburden what's weighing on the soul.

You don't have to be religious to feel it, and you don't have to be trained to recognize it. Something in us pushes toward honesty when something isn't right inside. We feel the weight of what we've done, and we instinctively look for somewhere to put that weight down (Prov. 28:13).

It's why New York City once had a confession hotline called the Apology Line. It was a real number people could call to admit what they'd done. No advice. No judgment. Just a place to release something heavy. Tens of thousands of people called the number over fifteen years.[3] That tells you something: Confession isn't just a moral act; it's a human need.

You see this in Catholic tradition too. The sacrament of confession isn't built on shame; it's built on the belief that naming what's broken helps heal what's broken.[4] Even psychology confirms what Scripture has been saying for thousands of years: Unconfessed guilt sits in the body. It shows up as anxiety, irritability, tension, depression, insomnia ... even physical pain.[5]

We aren't built to carry secrets indefinitely.

It's why a person will sometimes confess to a crime no one has solved yet. Not because confessing benefits them (it doesn't) but because withholding the truth slowly erodes the soul. Something in us wants to come clean.

So yes, we're wired to confess.

But the real question is: Confess to whom? And is it enough to confess on a horizontal level only?

Intuitively, something inside us tells us the answer to that question is no. And that's because, although horizontal confession releases pressure, vertical confession removes the stains (James 5:16; 1 John 1:9).

This is exactly what David understood in Psalm 51 when he said, "Against You, You only, have I sinned" (v. 4). David wasn't denying the real harm his sin had caused others; he was recognizing that beneath every horizontal offense lies a deeper, vertical one. Now, I know David was writing in Hebrew, not Greek. But I love the way the New Testament later captures this same idea with the Greek word often translated "confess"—*homologéō*—which means "to say the same thing or to agree with."[6] That concept helps clarify what David was doing here.

David was confessing that he was standing in total agreement with God, acknowledging *two things at once*:

- The nature of what he had done—that it was truly sin (vv. 3–4).
- The impact of what he had done—that ultimately every sin is an offense against God Himself (v. 4).

Something happens in vertical confession that never happens in horizontal confession: He cleanses us (1 John 1:9). And that's the win. We don't confess just to feel lighter but also to be forgiven.

Not to confess and feel relieved but to be restored (Ps. 51:7).

Confession is not about information.

It's about agreement.

Them—Rebuttal

Okay, but if I've already asked God to forgive me, why keep confessing the same sins?

You—Affirm

You're right in the sense that, once you've placed your faith in Christ, your sins are fully forgiven. Romans 8:1 says, "There is therefore now no condemnation to those who are in Christ Jesus." That's judicial forgiveness, the kind that removes guilt and declares you righteous once and for all.

Empathize

You've asked another great question, and it shows you actually care about how this works. It can feel like overkill to keep bringing up things that God has already forgiven.

Ask

So why keep confessing? Why does Scripture still call us to walk in repentance, even after salvation?

Answer

Because while judicial forgiveness deals with your standing before God, what we're talking about here is something we might call "parental" forgiveness, and it deals with your fellowship with Him (Rom. 5:1; 1 John 1:6–7).

Think about it like this: When my child disobeys me, they don't stop being my child. The relationship is still intact, but the fellowship is strained until the issue is resolved. Confession restores that closeness. It doesn't re-earn salvation; it reopens connection (Heb. 12:5–11).

That's exactly what John meant when he wrote: "If we say that we have fellowship with Him, and walk in darkness, we lie and do not practice the truth" (1 John 1:6).

Forgiveness in the legal sense is already completed. It was sealed at the cross (Col. 2:13–14; Heb. 10:10–14).

But intimacy, peace, and fellowship are daily realities that require ongoing humility and honesty before God (Ps. 66:18; James 4:8).

Jesus illustrated this when He washed the disciples' feet. When Peter protested, Jesus said, "Those who have had a bath need only to wash their feet; their whole body is clean" (John 13:10 NIV).

In other words: You're already forgiven, but you still need cleansing for daily dust (1 John 1:7).

That's what confession does.

- It keeps the relationship alive.
- It keeps love unhindered.
- It keeps the heart bent in the right direction.

KEYS FOR THE CONVERSATION

Every chapter has a lot of moving pieces, but if you can remember these keys, you'll carry the heart of this chapter and the tools you'll need into every conversation.

1. What You Need to Know

The need to be right is never about truth; it's only about you. It's a heart-posture problem. Because it's driven by ego instead of God, it becomes counterproductive, bending conversations toward dominance and self-protection instead of toward Him.

2. What You Need to Do

Read, memorize, and apply key scriptures related to pride and self-righteousness.

Find resources that speak directly to ego, identity, and humility.

Go to therapy, since these patterns are often deep rooted.

Practice *not* being right in everyday, low-stakes conversations so you can build the muscle before the hard ones arrive.

3. Who You Need to Become

Become someone willing to be wrong or simply to not know. Willing to learn. Someone who intends to win *the person*, not the argument.

Chapter 10

THE HOLY SPIRIT AND EVANGELISM

The Holy Spirit is the most important person on earth. Without Him, we have power without force and words without authority.

In the spirit of Myles Munroe

Restoring the Missing Piece

We cannot take the Holy Spirit out of our spiritual work and still call it spiritual. To detach the Spirit from evangelism is to mistake information for revelation, persuasion for conversion, and strategy for power. We can refine our arguments, master our methods, and polish our presentations, but without the Spirit, we have windless sails. We may move minds, but we will never move heaven or the human heart.

The Spirit of the Age

Paul was not being poetic when he referred to "the god of this age" (2 Cor. 4:4) or "the prince of the power of the air" (Eph. 2:2). He was describing a spiritual ecosystem, an invisible order of ideas, values, and influences that shape the visible world. It's what theologians and philosophers through the centuries have called the spirit of the age, the zeitgeist.

The term "the spirit of the age" is about more than cultural moods or generational trends. Biblically, the idea refers to the collective spiritual influence that animates human ideologies, moral reasoning, and cultural direction. It's not random or chaotic. It's coordinated, strategic, and deeply intellectual.

Behind every "new idea" that seeks to redefine God, truth, morality, or humanity, there's often an ancient intelligence at work. Paul makes this explicit:

> We wrestle not against flesh and blood, but against principalities, against powers, against the rulers of the darkness of this world, against spiritual wickedness in high places. (Eph. 6:12 KJV)

In modern terms, the devil is not merely a tempter; he's also a theologian and a philosopher. He traffics in ideas, worldviews, and language. His greatest weapon has never been force; it's always been persuasion (Gen. 3:1–5; John 8:44; 2 Cor. 11:3).

In Genesis 3, the serpent didn't appear in a blaze of demonic power; he came as a conversationalist. His weapon wasn't an attack but a question: "Did God really say ... ?" (v. 1 NIV).

That moment in the garden wasn't just humanity's moral fall; it was also the beginning of intellectual warfare. It launched a battle of words, definitions, and reasoning (Gen. 3:1–7; 2 Cor. 10:3–5). Satan didn't tempt Eve to hate God; he tempted her to reinterpret Him (Gen. 3:4–5; John 8:44).

From that point forward, every distortion of truth—whether religious, philosophical, or cultural—has followed the same pattern: a subtle redefinition of what God has said.

This is why Paul doesn't warn against sin only; he also warns against arguments. "We demolish arguments and every pretension that sets itself up against the knowledge of God" (2 Cor. 10:5 NIV). The Greek word behind "arguments" (*logismós*) refers to reasonings, systems of thought, or intellectual frameworks.[1]

That's where the real battle takes place. The enemy doesn't merely attack behavior; he targets belief itself—shaping how we think about God before we ever act in response to Him. Scripture warns us that the conflict is intellectual and spiritual, a war of ideas and frameworks that exalt themselves against the knowledge of God (2 Cor. 10:5).

This is the essence of the spirit of the age. It isn't hostile to religion as much as it is resistant to revelation. The goal is not to erase God but to redefine Him. That's why when Paul addressed the philosophers on Mars Hill, he wasn't indulging intellectual curiosity; he was confronting the spiritual architecture of a city shaped by competing narratives about truth, meaning, and authority.

The same is true today.

Every idea is built on an altar. Secularism, progressivism, consumerism, and nationalism are all sustained by belief systems that carry moral and spiritual assumptions. That's why Paul said, "Though we walk in the flesh, we do not war after the flesh" (2 Cor. 10:3 KJV). The visible conflict—arguments, policies, cultural movements—is only the surface. The real war is happening underneath.

Our age, like every age, has its own spirit: its preferred narrative about truth, identity, and meaning. The spirit of our modern age teaches that truth is subjective, identity is self-created, and morality is fluid. These ideas aren't just philosophical; they're spiritual. They form a worldview that blinds the mind from seeing the light of the gospel (2 Cor. 4:4).

And I don't doubt that in all the moments I've faced a crisis of faith, the same whisperer was at work. I understand the naturalistic arguments, and I believe that human depravity (the heart's tendency to pull away from God) plays a massive role in our unbelief.

Still, when I look back at the seasons when I was wrestling with faith, questioning what was true, weighing ancient claims against modern criticisms, whether grappling with copycat theories about Christianity or feeling abandoned by the very God I preached about, it's not lost on me that the whisperer was present there too. His tongue still spoke violence against truth. His logic was as ancient as Eden: subtle, sophisticated, and relentless. What I once mistook as purely intellectual wrestling was, at times, spiritual resistance.

That's why evangelism and our engagement with others can't be just intellectual. It must be spiritual. We're not just persuading minds; we're contending for hearts that have been subtly discipled by darkness.

Navigating the World of Ideas

If the spirit of the age has flooded the world with counterfeit wisdom, then modern life is its marketplace. Step into Times Square or the Las Vegas Strip, and you'll feel it immediately—screens screaming for attention, neon truths competing for belief, stories flashing faster than discernment can process.

That's the modern mind. Every scroll, headline, algorithm, and influencer is evangelizing for some worldview. The world of ideas has become a digital coliseum where ideologies fight for followers.

And yet, amid the blinding lights and noise, the Christian still bears a sacred responsibility to think clearly, love deeply, and speak wisely.

But that's impossible without the Holy Spirit.

When it comes to complicated conversations, we need God's Spirit for four things: power, poise, protection, and prompting. These four P's are essential. Because apologetics without anointing may win arguments but will never win hearts.

Before We Go Further—A Brief Look Back

In order to explore those four P's, it's important to remember that there has long been tension around the Holy Spirit. The church has wrestled with His role, nature, and operation for centuries.

The early church struggled to define His identity, leading to some of the most significant theological debates in history. Imagine being a believer then—watching leaders argue over whether the Spirit was divine, whether He was distinct from the Father and Son, or whether He was merely a force. The questions were real, and so were the divisions.

At the Council of Nicaea (AD 325), the divinity of the Holy Spirit was affirmed, though His exact relationship to the Father and Son remained somewhat undefined. Decades later, the Council of

Constantinople (AD 381) declared Him fully God, co-equal with the Father and the Son. Then came the Filioque Controversy (6th–11th centuries), when Christians debated whether the Spirit proceeds from the Father alone or from both the Father and the Son.[2]

It's easy to look back and think, *How could they not see what's so obvious?* But in truth, we're still having the same debates today. Who is the Holy Spirit? What is His role in the believer's life? Are the gifts of the Spirit still active, or did they cease with the early apostles?

Not long ago, my good friend Canton Jones and I had a two-hour conversation about the Holy Spirit. He shared some thought-provoking views—some I agreed with, others I didn't. But what I loved most was the exchange itself. It reminded me that even now, we're still wrestling to understand the Spirit's work. If we had lived in another era, maybe Canton's perspective would've been one of the ideas debated in a church council.

From the miracles and prophecy of the early church to the mysticism of the medieval era and the intellectual rigor of the Reformation, each generation has emphasized a facet of the Spirit's work. The twentieth century revived this conversation through global renewal movements.

- The Azusa Street Revival (1906): William J. Seymour, a one-eyed African American preacher, led an interracial outpouring in Los Angeles that birthed modern Pentecostalism.[3]
- The Charismatic Movement (1960s–1970s): Pentecostal experiences spread into mainline Protestant and Catholic churches.[4]

- The Third Wave (1980s–present): This era bridged Pentecostal fervor with evangelical restraint, affirming the gifts while insisting on order and maturity.[5]

Yet alongside every authentic move of God, charlatans and counterfeits have emerged—staging miracles, exploiting emotions, and commercializing the supernatural. That's why so many believers have grown cautious, even cynical, about the Spirit's power. But the existence of counterfeits proves that there's something real worth imitating. Nobody makes cubic zirconia unless there are diamonds to try to copy. But just because there is a counterfeit doesn't mean the real thing doesn't exist.

When cessationists argue that supernatural gifts were for a specific time and purpose, I understand. The Bible indeed shows the Spirit working uniquely in certain moments. Tongues, for instance, had a distinct function. In Acts 2, the disciples miraculously spoke in known languages that Jews from every nation understood. This wasn't emotional display; it was evangelistic evidence, a sign to unbelieving Jews that the gospel transcended boundaries of language, ethnicity, and status.

Some gifts, like tongues when the church was new, served as divine markers confirming that the gospel had crossed into new territories. But that does not mean the Spirit's work was confined to that age. The Holy Spirit hasn't retired from His post. He's still empowering believers, confirming truth, and transforming hearts.

We still see healings, prophetic insights, and encounters that bring people to faith. God's power was never about spectacle; it was about validation. Miracles functioned as apologetic events—visible arguments for invisible realities. And they still do.

Today, there's a hunger rising for more. People aren't merely seeking intellectual proofs; they're yearning for personal encounter. Across the world, in prayer rooms and secular spaces alike, hearts are crying for transcendence. Skeptics may scoff, but they should recall that even Jesus used miracles to draw people in. They didn't guarantee belief, but they invited it. In our age of deconstruction and doubt, we must recover that invitation—a gospel that is both reasoned and revealed.

The Four P's

Beyond the debates of history and the abuses of modern excess, one truth remains: We cannot fulfill Christ's mission without the Spirit who animates. If we are to engage a skeptical world that is marked by both intellectual pride and spiritual famine, we must rediscover what it means to rely on the Holy Spirit in every facet of evangelism and defense of the faith. In practical terms, this means cultivating the four P's: power, poise, protection, and prompting—four ways the Spirit equips believers to speak truth with conviction, humility, and divine authority.

Power

We need the Holy Spirit's power because ideas alone don't change people—encounters with the Spirit of God do.

Jesus promised, "You will receive power when the Holy Spirit has come upon you, and you will be my witnesses" (Acts 1:8 ESV). That word "power" (*dúnamis*) is not metaphorical.[6] It means real, demonstrative force; it is living proof that God is still active in the world.

I believe in signs and wonders. I believe that God's miraculous work can serve as an apologetic in itself. When the Spirit moves, skeptics notice. I've seen it in rooms where the Word was preached and the air shifted, where hardened faces softened, where cynics were arrested mid-thought by something they couldn't explain. I've watched people walk in expecting entertainment ... and leave in tears, unable to shake the sense that they had been seen.

Ideas alone don't change people—encounters with the Spirit of God do.

That's the supernatural dimension of truth. Paul wrote, "My speech and my preaching were not with persuasive words of human wisdom, but in demonstration of the Spirit and of power" (1 Cor. 2:4). He didn't reject intellect ... he simply knew that intellect wasn't enough. The Holy Spirit doesn't compete with reason; He completes it.

And this power isn't limited to miracles or healing. It's also the power to stand in hostile spaces with conviction, to endure ridicule without retreat, to love your enemies in public discourse, to stay faithful when everything in the culture says you're foolish, and to overcome evil with good.

It takes supernatural strength to remain truthful and tender in the same sentence. That's the power of the Holy Ghost.

Missionaries have seen it, pastors have felt it, artists have expressed it. In every generation, the gospel has advanced not merely through clever words but also through the arresting presence of God. The same

Spirit who raised Christ from the dead still moves hearts today—and sometimes, His movement is the most persuasive argument of all.

Poise

If power is what gives us courage, poise is what keeps us composed.

In an age of outrage, the fruit of the Spirit is the new apologetic. Love, joy, peace, patience, kindness, goodness, faithfulness, gentleness, and self-control are not personality traits—they are proof of transformation.

But the fruit of the Spirit is often misunderstood. Though it's listed as nine virtues in Galatians 5:22–23, Paul uses the singular form of the word: fruit, not fruits. That means it's not a basket of spiritual produce where you can pick and choose—love one day, patience the next, for example. It's more like a smoothie than a fruit bowl. Each virtue is blended together, inseparable, forming one composite expression of Christ's character.

It takes supernatural strength to remain truthful and tender in the same sentence. That's the power of the Holy Ghost.

The fruit of the Spirit is what happens when divine life grows in human soil. But I used to wonder: If that's true, why do I see non-Christians who seem just as kind, patient, or joyful as Christians—sometimes even more so? I've seen atheists who show incredible self-control. I've met skeptics who exude generosity. How does that make sense?

Where I've landed is this: We're all made in the image of God. So it's not strange that an atheist might display some of His attributes. Every human being bears traces of divine likeness. But that image, though beautiful, is broken—it's like a cracked mirror that still reflects light.

The difference is this: The Holy Spirit doesn't merely reflect virtue; He produces it.

Paul said, "Be not drunk with wine ... but be filled with the Spirit" (Eph. 5:18 KJV). The comparison is intentional. Wine is a disinhibitor—it causes people to say or do things they wouldn't naturally say or do. In the same way, the Spirit empowers believers to live beyond what is natural.

So yes, a person without God can be patient—but the Spirit enables supernatural patience when we're wronged. Someone without faith can be kind, but the Spirit empowers kindness even toward our enemies. Self-control, joy, gentleness ... these are not natural dispositions; they're divine interventions. They manifest most clearly in our weakness, in the moments when flesh would fail.

That's why Paul ties the fruit of the Spirit to dependency. It's not behavior modification—it's spiritual transformation. It's not "try harder"; it's "yield deeper." When we are filled with the Spirit, we are carried beyond the limitations of personality, temperament, and willpower. The fruit becomes the evidence of the indwelling presence of God.

And that's what makes poise possible. The Spirit gives us the composure to face ridicule, the calm to withstand hostility, and the joy to stay centered in chaos. Poise is not pretending you're unaffected—it's being anchored by Someone greater than your emotions.

In many ways, it's what makes truth believable. A poised Christian can disagree without being disagreeable. They can confront without condemning and stand firm without raising their voice.

Jesus embodied this perfectly before Pilate, utter composure in the face of injustice (John 19:8–12).

I think of the countless public figures who remain calm under pressure—leaders, speakers, and communicators who field tension, criticism, or conflict with remarkable composure. You've probably seen someone who is clearly not a person of faith confronted unexpectedly, yet their tone stays level and their posture steady. Whether on a stage, in an interview, or in a moment of challenge, they model a natural poise that stabilizes the room.

What that says to me is, *If human temperament alone can produce that kind of steadiness, how much more should believers, filled with the Spirit, be marked by supernatural calm?*

The Holy Spirit gives us that balance—truth with tenderness, conviction with composure, boldness without brashness. And yet, even that balance is only part of what we need. Because the moment we step into real conversations about faith, we're entering something far deeper than dialogue. When we engage culture as evangelists and apologists, we're not just debating worldviews, we are confronting spiritual strategies that have been at work long before we were born. As I mentioned earlier, Paul the apostle writes, "The weapons of our warfare are not carnal but mighty in God for pulling down strongholds, casting down arguments and every high thing that exalts itself against the knowledge of God" (2 Cor. 10:4–5).

The word Paul uses for "arguments" (*logismós*) refers to structured reasoning, calculated patterns of thought; worldviews that have been built, reinforced, and refined over time.[7] In other words, we are not just responding to random opinions but to intellectual formations designed to stand against the truth of God.

Which means we cannot contend with a supernatural adversary using natural weapons.

We are up against an enemy who is ancient, intelligent, strategic, and deeply familiar with human nature. Scripture names him plainly: *the accuser, the deceiver, the adversary.* He has watched humanity long enough to understand what we desire, what we fear, and where we are weak.

This is why we can't rely on intellect, logic, or training alone. Those things matter—they matter immensely—but by themselves, they are insufficient. We need the Spirit of God because we are confronting ideologies that are spiritually animated, narratives that are spiritually charged, and arguments that are spiritually fortified.

Paul reminds us again: "We wrestle not against flesh and blood, but against principalities, against powers, against the rulers of the darkness of this world, against spiritual wickedness in high places" (Eph. 6:12 KJV).

Our adversary is not a human being who is a content creator, philosopher, skeptic, or atheist. Our adversary is the devil. And the ideologies that distort truth in our generation are not merely human, either; they are *influenced by spiritual forces* that resist the revelation of Christ.

This is why the Spirit is indispensable.

He empowers us not only to speak with wisdom but also to stand with authority, to discern deception, to respond with truth, and to confront falsehood without losing compassion. He gives us insight beyond research, discernment beyond instinct, and strength beyond personality.

In a world filled with intellectual strongholds, philosophical resistance, and spiritual opposition, the Holy Spirit is not optional ... He is essential.

Protection

We also need the Holy Spirit for protection.

Because make no mistake: Ideas are not neutral. Every podcast, post, or philosophy carries seeds. Some grow faith; others grow doubt. And if our hearts are unguarded, the soil of our soul can easily be overtaken by weeds.

Proverbs 4:23 warns, "Above all else, guard your heart, for everything you do flows from it" (NIV). The Holy Spirit is that guard. He protects us as we engage with, listen to, and absorb the constant stream of narratives shaping the world around us.

Even those of us who love Scripture are not immune. Anyone can drift. Anyone can deconstruct. All it takes is a seed—the same kind the serpent planted in Eden: "Did God really say ...?" That's why we can't engage the culture without also anchoring ourselves in prayer, consecration, and communion.

And perhaps one of the greatest dangers, especially for mature believers, is overestimating our own strength. It's easy to assume we're beyond deception or that spiritual maturity makes us less vulnerable. But Peter proves otherwise. When Jesus warned him that he would deny Him, Peter pushed back, insisting, "Even if all fall away, I will not" (Mark 14:29 NIV). He overestimated his strength when Jesus predicted his denial, and he did it again when Jesus told him, "Watch and pray so that you will not fall into temptation" (Matt. 26:41 NIV). Instead of praying, Peter slept. And in the moment of testing, he proved Jesus exactly right.

And listen, I know this firsthand. I've been Peter more than once. I've overestimated my strength and underestimated my weakness. I've assumed I could handle temptation, pressure, or discouragement on my own. It's something I've had to learn the hard way, and something I still guard against intentionally. I don't read Peter's story as an indictment; I read it as a mirror. It's a reminder that even the strongest among us can fall asleep when we should be praying.

That's the subtle trap of spiritual confidence: It feels like faith but often masks presumption. The truth is, no one outgrows dependence on the Holy Spirit. The moment we assume we're beyond falling is the moment our guard drops. And in an age as intellectually and spiritually seductive as ours, that's a dangerous place to be.

Prayer waters the seed of righteousness that God has planted through His Word. It keeps the soil soft and the roots deep. The fruit of the Spirit (love, joy, peace, self-control, and the rest) isn't born in the moment of argument; it's cultivated beforehand in the hidden life of devotion. It is a mistake to think we can simply "turn on" the Spirit's fruit when we find ourselves in crisis. Joy, gentleness, and self-control must be formed before they're tested.

That's why daily prayer and regular consecration aren't legalistic duties; they're means of grace. They keep the heart guarded and the mind renewed. In a world that's constantly sowing distraction, fear, and self-worship, the Spirit fortifies us with discernment, humility, and holy resilience.

Prompting

Sometimes, in unpredictable moments, the Holy Spirit simply gives us the words.

Jesus promised it: "Do not worry about how to respond or what to say.... For it will not be you speaking, but the Spirit of your Father speaking through you" (Matt. 10:19–20 BSB).

There are times when preparation can't keep up with Providence. When the conversation takes a turn you didn't anticipate, and suddenly a word, an image, a Scripture rises in your spirit—custom fit for that person. You can't plan it; you can't fake it. It's divine improvisation.

Hart Ramsey calls it "mouth-to-ear ministry"—the Spirit downloads heaven's wisdom straight into your vocabulary. I've experienced it; most believers have. It's the moment when the line between your words and His becomes almost invisible.

Those moments remind us that evangelism is never mechanical. It's relational—between God, us, and the person He loves.

In a world overflowing with noise, we need the Holy Spirit to empower us, center us, protect us, and speak through us. Without Him, we're just another voice in the static. *With* Him, every word carries weight, every act of love bears witness, and every conversation becomes a chance for heaven to interrupt earth.

CURIOUS CONVERSATION

"Is the devil real or imagined?"

In this chapter, I've talked about how much of what we wrestle with in evangelism happens beneath the surface. And by that, I don't simply mean matters of personality or identity, but the deeper currents that shape how people interpret reality itself. Most people, whether they admit it or not, have an intuition that there is more going on in the world than what meets the eye.

What's fascinating is how that intuition has been muted in a culture shaped by naturalism. Even when people sense that our struggle runs deeper than psychology or circumstance alone, the language they reach for reflects a hesitation to name anything beyond the material.

We experience this in everyday culture when people talk about "demons," not as literal spirits but as metaphors for trauma, addiction, or inner battles: "He's fighting his demons" or "Those are my inner devils." The language is poetic, but it gives something away. Even when belief in a literal Satan is absent, evil is still experienced as personal.

Possible Dialogue

Them—Objection

I don't even believe the devil exists. Religion invented this figure to make sense of the evil in the world.

You—Rude Response

Okay, well, I guess you'll believe when it's too late.

Why This Doesn't Work

It sounds smug. And people who see the devil as a myth aren't usually being dismissive. To them, believing in Satan feels like believing in Zeus or Hades. Instead of being "clever," meet them where they actually are.

Better Response

You—Affirm

I get that. I've seen a lot of ex-Christians touting that idea.

Empathize

Honestly, I've never thought that way. But in a culture that leans heavily on rationalism and evidence-based thinking, it makes sense why you'd see it that way.

Ask

Do you believe in God? If so, what do you believe about His nature? Is He pure and good or not?

Answer

I ask because, if you don't believe in the existence of God, then disbelieving in the devil makes perfect sense. However, if God exists, and if He is the very essence of goodness and the reason for all that is good in the world, then it's not unreasonable to conclude that there is also a real spiritual opposition to that goodness. God is the ultimate source of light, love, and truth. Yet the world is undeniably dark, destructive, and deceptive.

If good exists and is spiritual, then evil must be its spiritual counterpart. Not equal in power, but opposite in nature.

And biblically, this is what we see Jesus saying. Jesus spoke to and confronted this being directly. He called him "the father of lies" (John 8:44 NIV). He cast out demons. He said, "I saw Satan fall like lightning from heaven" (Luke 10:18). The devil's name itself means "accuser."[8]

To deny his existence is to ignore the possibility that evil is not just what we do but also what drives what we do.

Them—Rebuttal 1

Even if he's real, why do Christians blame him for everything?

You—Affirm

That's a fair critique. Christians do sometimes overspiritualize things, blaming the devil for everything from a flat tire to a bad day.

Empathize

I get how that looks from the outside. It can sound like we're dodging accountability or projecting blame.

Ask

Would you say it's natural for people, whether religious or not, to look for someone or something outside themselves to blame when they mess up or suffer?

Answer

I would say blame shifting is human nature. It's what Adam did in Genesis 3:12 and what we still do today. But biblically, the devil's existence doesn't erase human responsibility. So yes, the devil is real, and there are some atrocities in history so deep, so systematic, so "superhuman," that they seem to go beyond human nature itself. But not every mistake or sin is his doing. People tend to swing to extremes, either ignoring him completely (2 Cor. 2:11) or blaming him for everything.

The balanced view is that we live in a both/and world:

- Human choices are real (Deut. 30:19).
- Spiritual opposition is real (Eph. 6:12).
- God's sovereignty still stands above both (Isa. 46:9–10).

Them—Rebuttal 2

Okay, but if the devil exists, is he equal to God?

You—Affirm

That's a great question, because a lot of people think of God and the devil like two equal opposites: light vs. dark, yin and yang.

Empathize

Sometimes it feels that way. The darkness in the world can seem so overwhelming that it feels like evil must be God's equal.

Ask

Do you think of God and the devil as kind of a yin and yang?

Answer

The devil is not God's equal opposite.

- He is God's creation who rebelled (Rev. 12:7–9).
- We see that clearly in Job: Satan has to ask permission before he can act (Job 1:6–12).
- In James, we're told that demons believe in God ... and tremble (James 2:19).
- Paul says that every being in heaven, on earth, and under the earth will confess that Jesus is Lord (Phil. 2:10–11).
- And in the Gospels, demons ask Jesus, "Have you come here to torture us before the appointed time?" (Matt. 8:29 NIV; see also Luke 8:31).
- So yes, the devil is powerful, far beyond human capacity, but he is still limited, finite, and defeated. He is not omnipresent (1 Pet. 5:8), not omniscient (Matt. 24:36), and not omnipotent (Rev. 20:1–3).
- He's spirit but not sovereign (Eph. 2:2; Dan. 4:35).
- He's cunning but not creative (Gen. 3:1; John 8:44).
- He's terrifying but already triumphed over (John 12:31; Col. 2:15).

The entire biblical narrative shows that Satan's power is temporary and tethered. The same Jesus who faced him in the wilderness will ultimately destroy him in judgment (Rev. 20:10). Evil still rages, but it's fighting a losing battle against a God whose authority it cannot match. Belief in the devil isn't superstition; it's realism. Evil has intelligence, persistence, and personality (John 8:44). God is good, God is spirit, and if the world He made is not currently good, then the most coherent explanation is that there exists a spiritual force opposed to God's goodness. He's real, but he's not equal. And he's already been outmatched (1 John 4:4).

KEYS FOR THE CONVERSATION

Every chapter has a lot of moving pieces, but if you can remember these keys, you'll carry the heart of this chapter and the tools you'll need into every conversation.

1. What You Need to Know

Evangelism is never a solo act. The Holy Spirit is the one who convicts, draws, softens, awakens, and opens the heart. In the act of evangelism, you are responsible for *faithfulness*, not perfection.

When you understand that you are *not alone* in high-stakes conversations, that the Holy Spirit Himself is present and active, the pressure to get every word right begins to lift. This isn't a work powered by human effort. "'Not by might nor by power, but by My Spirit,' says the LORD" (Zech. 4:6). Remember that.

2. What You Need to Do

Pray before you speak. Pray *while* you speak. Pray after you speak.

Stay sensitive to His prompting on when to be quiet, when to press in, when to speak boldly, and when to simply plant a seed and step back.

Depend on the Spirit more than your strategy.

3. Who You Need to Become

Become someone who places the weight of your confidence on the presence of the Spirit of God. Someone whose life is defined and continually shaped by practicing His presence. Someone who carries a balanced but heavy reliance on His power, understanding that the primary work of the Holy Spirit is to point people to Jesus.

CONCLUSION

Forgive Me If I Was Rude isn't just a title; it's a confession from someone who has stumbled through conversations, learned from missteps, and continues to grow. I've reacted too quickly at times, spoken too sharply, misunderstood the moment, or carried my own assumptions into places where they didn't belong. I've had to apologize, reflect, and reset more times than I can count. I'm still doing that.

But this book isn't simply a compilation of personal stories. It's also the fruit of years of study, training, research, and engagement with complex questions shaping our cultural moment. It's the meeting place of both versions of me: the student still being made wiser through hard conversations and the scholar-practitioner equipped to guide others through them.

Looking Back

Throughout these chapters, we explored the inner and outer work of meaningful conversations—the posture, the awareness, the timing, the humility, the patience, the spiritual grounding. We learned how to read the room, how to see the person, how to check our assumptions, and how to understand the cultural and emotional forces shaping the moment.

We looked at how body language speaks before your words ever do. How doubt can be handled with compassion. How disagreement doesn't require disrespect. How humility guards your heart. How boldness can be clear without being cruel. And how the Holy Spirit meets you in real time, in real conversations, with real people.

And we've seen several step-by-step walk-throughs of how to respond when people ask real questions in real situations. The approach. The patterns. The pivots. The questions—the "cheat code."

Looking Forward

The reality is that once you're done reading this book, you'll be stepping back into a world that is loud, divided, easily angered, and deeply wounded. A world where people speak before thinking, react before listening, and assume before understanding. A world where people are easily triggered and conversations can feel like landmines.

But you are not stepping into that world empty-handed.

You now carry a way of seeing, listening, discerning, slowing down, and showing up that is different. It's a way shaped by wisdom, softened by humility, strengthened by clarity, and animated by the Holy Spirit.

You're now stepping into conversations with the *confidence*, *clarity*, and *language* to engage hard and complicated conversations with *dignity*, *love*, and *respect*.

So as you go, use your tools and trust the work God is doing in you.

You won't get it right every time. Neither will I.

But every conversation is another chance to practice the kind of presence that makes Jesus visible.

ACKNOWLEDGMENTS

I owe everything I am and everything I've become to my parents, Emanuel Lambert Sr. and Martina Lambert, first.

From the very beginning, they stoked the fire of faith in me. They raised me to fear the Lord, to love His Word, and to pursue truth with both heart and mind. While other kids were memorizing nursery rhymes, they had me memorizing Scripture. By five years old, I was standing in front of the church reciting verses. As a child, I was surrounded by biblical stories on cassette, Sunday sermons, and my father's commentaries stacked on the table. By the time I was a teenager, my parents had cultivated in me not just belief but an appetite for God, theology, and learning. That hunger has shaped every part of my life. For that, I'm eternally grateful.

To the men who helped form and sharpen me over the years—thank you.

Dave Thomas, who was once my youth pastor and later became a discipler, a brother, and a friend—you helped shape the way I think about God and the practical matters of life, relationships, purpose, and wisdom. You saw something in me early on that maybe I didn't see in myself. You introduced me to Bible college, and that single act changed the entire direction of my life.

William "The Ambassador" Branch, who was indeed my father in the faith—you discipled me, taught me, molded me, shaped me, and rooted and established me in the most holy faith. You taught me the way of Christ. You opened my eyes to the seriousness of the Christian journey—to the call to be on mission. You showed me how to integrate and marry my faith, my craft, and my culture. Forever grateful to you. I watched you night after night on stage as we toured with The Cross Movement, and I soaked in every word you spoke. I tried to talk like you, dress like you, and think like you. Your impact on my theology, my perspective, and my understanding of who Jesus is runs deep to this day.

Bishop Ellis, my pastor in Philadelphia at Victory Christian Center Church—thank you for modeling apostolic authority with humility, being a teacher of the Word, and restoring me during one of the darkest seasons of my life.

Pastor Hart Ramsey, one of the most brilliant and prophetic minds I know—thank you for walking with me through turbulent seasons, and for your wisdom, your friendship, and your relentless insistence on integrity and growth.

Sam Collier, my brother for life—thank you for always putting the battery in my back. You fought with me in the foxhole and stood with me in the trenches. You pushed me to dream bigger, fly higher, and believe that what God placed in me deserves to live. You've been beside me in every climb, every pivot, every reinvention.

To my wife, **Briana Lambert**, my heart and home—thank you for holding it all together while I wrote this book. For eleven months, you carried the weight with me. You made sure I had my double espresso shots when I was up for seventy-two hours straight, running on fumes and vision. You created the space for me to lock in and pour out everything God put inside me. You are my greatest support, my covering, and the incentive for me to keep going, even when I'm weary.

And finally, to every supporter who's been with me through every season—thank you. Through every album, every reinvention, every high and low, you've stayed. You've grown with me from artist to apologist, from musician to messenger, and now from artist to author. I'm excited for what's ahead.

Thank you for believing.

ABOUT THE AUTHOR

Born and raised in West Philadelphia, Da' T.R.U.T.H. (Emanuel Lee Lambert, Jr.) has spent more than two decades using music, teaching, and apologetics to engage culture and inspire faith. A respected voice in Christian music and ministry, he has built a career marked by artistic excellence, theological depth, and a passion for helping people think critically about what they believe and why they believe it.

A multi-award-winning artist, Da' T.R.U.T.H. has received numerous accolades, including three Grammy Award nominations, three Dove Award nominations, and five Stellar Awards.

Throughout his career, he has sold nearly a quarter million records worldwide, recorded numerous acclaimed projects, and toured extensively across every continent. Having worked with artists ranging from Kirk Franklin, Mary Mary, Tye Tribbett, Jill Scott, Lecrae, and CeCe Winans, he has established himself as one of Christian music's most respected voices. His work has been featured on major platforms including MTV and BET, and he has appeared on some of the industry's biggest stages, including four performances on the Stellar Awards.

Beyond music, Da' T.R.U.T.H. is an accomplished teacher, apologist, and author. He is a graduate of Cairn University, a graduate of the Institute of Jewish Studies, and is certified in Christian Apologetics through the Oxford Centre for Christian Apologetics (OCCA). His academic training, combined with decades of ministry experience, has positioned him as a sought-after communicator on faith, culture, theology, worldview, and discipleship.

Over the course of more than twenty-five years in ministry, Da' T.R.U.T.H. has served as a teaching pastor, consultant, conference speaker, and ministry leader. He has worked alongside and served influential churches and ministries including Hillsong Church, Christian Cultural Center, and Relentless Church, partnering with respected leaders such as A.R. Bernard, John Gray, Hart Ramsey, Jamal Bryant, Sam Collier, and others. Through these opportunities, he has helped equip leaders, strengthen discipleship efforts, and engage audiences around some of Christianity's most challenging questions.

Today, Emanuel "Da' T.R.U.T.H." Lambert is the founder of Intelligent Faith, an apologetics ministry dedicated to helping believers develop an informed, thoughtful, and confident faith. Through music, teaching, writing, leadership development, and live events, he continues to challenge audiences to engage life's hardest questions with both conviction and compassion.

Through Intelligent Faith, Da' T.R.U.T.H. is helping a new generation move beyond inherited belief toward a faith that is informed, examined, and deeply rooted in truth.

NOTES

Introduction

1. R. P. C. Hanson, *The Search for the Christian Doctrine of God* (T&T Clark, 1988), 159–210.

2. Richard Price and Michael Gaddis, *The Acts of the Council of Chalcedon*, vol. 2. (Liverpool University Press, 2007).

Chapter 1

1. Andy Stanley, *Irresistible: Reclaiming the New That Jesus Unleashed for the World* (Zondervan, 2018), Kindle, 269.

2. N. T. Wright, *Paul: A Biography* (HarperOne, 2018).

3. Charles Swindoll, *Living on the Ragged Edge* (Thomas Nelson Incorporated, 1985), 14.

4. Wild Videos (@FightStorage), "Willow Smith sent out an 'important' PSA," repost of Willow Smith PSA on ascetic lifestyles (originally posted by @willow-smith, no longer available), X (formerly Twitter), April 4, 2026, https://x.com/FightStorage/status/2040625486917976448.

5. Plato, *Theaetetus*, ed. Myles Burnyeat, trans. M. J. Levett (Hackett Publishing, 1990).

6. George Orwell, *1984* (Secker & Warburg, 1949), 83.

7. Os Guinness, *The Global Public Square: Religious Freedom and the Making of a World Safe for Diversity*, (InterVarsity Press, 2013).

8. Charles Taylor, *A Secular Age* (Harvard University Press, 2007).

9. "Stress in America 2023: A Nation Recovering from Collective Trauma ," American Psychological Association, November 2023, www.apa.org/news/press/releases/stress/2023/collective-trauma-recovery.

Chapter 2

1. Michael J. Gorman, *Apostle of the Crucified Lord: A Theological Introduction to Paul and His Letters*, 2nd ed. (William B. Eerdmans, 2017).

2. Os Guinness, *A Free People's Suicide: Sustainable Freedom and the American Future* (InterVarsity Press, 2012).

3. Roy F. Baumeister et al., "Ego Depletion: Is the Active Self a Limited Resource?," *Journal of Personality and Social Psychology* 74, no. 5 (1998): 1252–65.

Chapter 3

1. Klyne Snodgrass, *Stories with Intent: A Comprehensive Guide to the Parables of Jesus* (Wm. B. Eerdmans Publishing, 2008).

2. "My Story," MP3 audio, track 6 on Emanuel "Da' T.R.U.T.H." Lambert, *Moment of Truth*, Cross Movement Records, 2004.

Chapter 4

1. David Propper, "Charlamagne tha God, Whoopi Goldberg Clash over Biden's Hunter Pardon on 'The View': 'Why Can't You Say When Democrats Are Wrong?,'" *New York Post*, December 4, 2024.

2. Albert Mehrabian and Morton Wiener, "Decoding of Inconsistent Communications," *Journal of Personality and Social Psychology* 6, no. 1 (1967): 109–14.

3. Craig S. Keener, *The IVP Bible Background Commentary: New Testament* (InterVarsity Press, 1993), 208–9.

4. F. E. Peters, *The Monotheists: Jews, Christians, and Muslims in Conflict and Competition* (Princeton University Press, 2003).

Chapter 5

1. F. E. Peters, *The Monotheists: Jews, Christians, and Muslims in Conflict and Competition* (Princeton University Press, 2003).

2. Walter Bauer, "εὐαγγέλιον," in *A Greek-English Lexicon of the New Testament and Other Early Christian Literature*, 4th ed., ed. Frederick William Danker (University of Chicago Press, 2021), 355.

3. John Dickson, *The Best Kept Secret of Christian Mission: Promoting the Gospel with More Than Our Lips* (Zondervan, 2010).

Chapter 6

1. DJ Akademiks, "DJ Akademiks & (Ye) Kanye West — Interview [Full] | Talks Drake, Kendrick Lamar, Playboi Cart & more," YouTube video, March 30, 2025, www.youtube.com/watch?v=F3Zt3rvgCcM.

2. Justo L. González, *The Story of Christianity*, vol. 1, *The Early Church to the Dawn of the Reformation*, rev. ed. (HarperOne, 2010).

3. Jackie Hill Perry, *Gay Girl, Good God: The Story of Who I Was, and Who God Has Always Been* (B&H Publishing Group, 2018).

4. Augustine, *The City of God*, ed. Gillian Rosemary, trans. Henry Bettenson (Penguin Classics, 2003), 858.

Chapter 7

1. Walter Bauer, "ἁγιάζω," in *A Greek-English Lexicon of the New Testament and Other Early Christian Literature*, 4th ed., ed. Frederick William Danker (University of Chicago Press, 2021), 8.

2. Princella Clark, @thequeenmakerofficial, "The male needs a male God," Instagram, June 16, 2025, www.instagram.com/p/DK9qVkYqTYH/

3. Martin Luther, "Two Kinds of Righteousness," in *Martin Luther's Basic Theological Writings*, ed. by Timothy F. Lull and William R. Russell (Fortress Press, 2012), 155–61.

4. "Euphoria," by Kendrick Lamar, written by Kenneth Gamble, Ronald LaTour, Daveon Lamont, et al., produced by Sounwave et al., Interscope Records, Universal Music Publishing, Warner Chappell Music, MP3 audio, released as a single April 30, 2024.

5. Jacob Neusner, *An Introduction to Judaism: A Textbook and Reader* (Westminster/John Knox Press, 1991).

Chapter 8

1. Joachim Jeremias, *Jerusalem in the Time of Jesus: An Investigation into Economic and Social Conditions During the New Testament Period* (Fortress Press, 1969), 312.

2. Craig S. Keener, *The IVP Bible Background Commentary: New Testament* (InterVarsity Press, 1993), 253–54.

3. Craig A. Evans, *Fabricating Jesus: How Modern Scholars Distort the Gospels* (InterVarsity Press, 2006).

4. Bruce M. Metzger, *The Canon of the New Testament: Its Origin, Development, and Significance* (Clarendon Press, 1987).

5. Homer, *The Odyssey*, trans. Robert Fagles (Penguin Classics, 1997).

6. Richard Bauckham, *Jesus and the Eyewitnesses: The Gospels as Eyewitness Testimony* (Wm. B. Eerdmans Publishing, 2006).

7. Richard Bauckham, *Jesus and the Eyewitnesses: The Gospels as Eyewitness Testimony*, 2nd ed. (Wm. B. Eerdmans Publishing, 2017).

8. F. F. Bruce, *The New International Commentary*, rev. ed., *The Book of the Acts* (Wm. B. Eerdmans Publishing, 1988).

9. F. F. Bruce, *New International Commentary, Book of Acts* (Grand Rapids: Eerdmans, 1988).

Chapter 9

1. C. S. Lewis, *Mere Christianity* (HarperCollins, 2001).

2. Augustine, *The City of God*, ed. Gillian Rosemary, trans. Henry Bettenson (Penguin Classics, 2003).

3. Fiona Sturges, "The Apology Line Podcast Tells the Story of a Phone Line for Confessions," *Financial Times*, January 24, 2021, www.ft.com/content/df1cc225-62e9-4993-8234-0f1713107f91.

4. United States Catholic Conference, *Catechism of the Catholic Church*, 2nd ed. (Libreria Editrice Vaticana, 1997).

5. James W. Pennebaker, *Opening Up: The Healing Power of Expressing Emotions* (Guilford Publications, 1997).

6. Walter Bauer, "ὁμολογέω," in *A Greek-English Lexicon of the New Testament and Other Early Christian Literature*, 4th ed., ed. Frederick William Danker (University of Chicago Press, 2021), 628.

Chapter 10

1. Walter Bauer, "λογισμός," in *A Greek-English Lexicon of the New Testament and Other Early Christian Literature*, 4th ed., ed. Frederick William Danker (University of Chicago Press, 2021), 530.

2. J. N. D. Kelly, *Early Christian Doctrines*, rev. ed. (HarperSanFrancisco, 1978).

3. Cecil M. Robeck Jr., *The Azusa Street Mission and Revival: The Birth of the Global Pentecostal Movement* (Thomas Nelson, 2006).

4. Vinson Synan, *The Holiness-Pentecostal Tradition: Charismatic Movements in the Twentieth Century*, 2nd ed. (Wm. B. Eerdmans Publishing, 1997).

5. C. Peter Wagner, *The Third Wave of the Holy Spirit: Encountering the Power of Signs and Wonders Today* (Vine Books, 1988).

6. Bauer, "δύναμις," in *Greek-English Lexicon*, 232.

7. Bauer, "λογισμός," in *Greek-English Lexicon*, 530.

8. "G1228–diabolos," *Strong's Concordance, Blue Letter Bible,* accessed June 19, 2026, www.blueletterbible.org/lexicon/g1228/ls/mgnt/43-1/.